Changing the American Schoolbook

Lexington Books Politics of Education Series
Frederick M. Wirt, Editor

Michael W. Kirst, Ed., *State, School, and Politics: Research Directions*

Joel S. Berke, Michael W. Kirst, *Federal Aid to Education: Who Benefits? Who Governs?*

Al J. Smith, Anthony Downs, M. Leanne Lachman, *Achieving Effective Desegregation*

Kern Alexander, K. Forbis Jordan, *Constitutional Reform of School Finance*

George R. LaNoue, Bruce L.R. Smith, *The Politics of School Decentralization*

David J. Kirby, T. Robert Harris, Robert L. Crain, Christine H. Rossell, *Political Strategies in Northern School Desegregation*

Philip K. Piele, John Stuart Hall, *Budgets, Bonds, and Ballots: Voting Behavior in School Financial Elections*

John C. Hogan, *The Schools, the Courts, and the Public Interest*

Jerome T. Murphy, *State Education Agencies and Discretionary Funds: Grease The Squeaky Wheel*

Howard Hamilton, Sylvan Cohen, *Policy-Making by Plebiscite: School Referenda*

Daniel J. Sullivan, *Public Aid to Nonpublic Schools*

James Hottois, Neal A. Milner, *The Sex Education Controversy: A Study of Politics, Education, and Morality*

Lauriston R. King, *The Washington Lobbyists for Higher Education*

Frederick M. Wirt, Ed., *The Polity of the School: New Research in Educational Politics*

Peter J. Cistone, Ed., *Understanding School Boards: Problems and Prospects*

Lawrence E. Gladieux, Thomas R. Wolanin, *Congress and the Colleges: The National Politics of Higher Education*

Dale Mann, *The Politics of Administrative Representation: School Administrators and Local Democracy*

Harrell R. Rodgers, Jr., Charles S. Bullock III, *Coercion to Compliance*

Richard A. Dershimer, *The Federal Government and Educational R&D*

Tyll van Geel, *Authority to Control the School Program*

Andrew Fishel, Janice Pottker, *National Politics and Sex Discrimination in Education*

Chester E. Finn, Jr., *Education and the Presidency*

Frank W. Lutz, Laurence Iannoccone, *Public Participation in Local School Districts*

Paul Goldstein, *Changing the American Schoolbook*

Changing the American Schoolbook

Law, Politics, and Technology

Paul Goldstein
Stanford Law School

Lexington Books
D.C. Heath and Company
Lexington, Massachusetts
Toronto

Library of Congress Cataloging in Publication Data

Goldstein, Paul, 1943–
   Changing the American schoolbook.

   Includes index.
   1. Text-books–United States. I. Title.
LB3047.G64   379'.156'0973   77-11572
ISBN 0-669-01984-4

To Jan

Contents

viii

Preface

This book asks a simple question: Why, after so many years and so much investment, have the American schoolbook, and instructional materials generally, changed so little? The answer is far from simple. Politics, economics and sociology offer some clues. So do the statutes and other legal rules governing federal subsidy programs, school selection of instructional materials and publisher investment in instructional materials research and development. The observed behavior of teachers and school systems also begins to explain the absence of change. Gathering and analyzing these clues and facts required the help of several institutions and many, many people. I am grateful to them all.

Mary Jean Bowman, Richard Markovits and Robert Rabin served as consultants to the study on which this book is based; each exhaustively reviewed the original study report. Colleagues at Stanford and elsewhere read all or portions of the manuscript in various stages of its development; comments from Richard Danzig, Richard Dershimer, Michael Kirst, Steven Klepper and Bruce Owen were particularly helpful. Morton Bachrach, Morton Goldberg, Arthur Livermore and Linda Sikorski helped with literature, leads and details that otherwise would have been inaccessible.

From the beginning of the research project to the completion of the book, I was aided by an extraordinarily industrious and gifted group of research assistants. At the State University of New York at Buffalo, where the research project began, I had the help of Martha Gordon, Joan Hollinger and Dianne McCarty. At Stanford, where the research and the book were completed, I had the help of Douglas Baird, Jonathan Kempner and Carol Roehl; their assistance was supported with funds made available by the Law School. One person, Bert Slonim, was involved with the project almost from its beginning to its completion; it is impossible for me to express the extent of my debt to him—for his generous assistance and good advice, and for the gift of his friendship throughout.

Barbara Laboch at Buffalo and Anne Diesel and Phyllis Stephens at Stanford typed a long succession of draft manuscripts carefully and without complaint. At Buffalo, Audrey Koscielniak coordinated budgetary matters effectively and graciously. At Stanford, Erika Kaltenbach was similarly gracious in helping work out the many details that cropped up between manuscript and press.

Some of the materials incorporated in this work were developed with the financial support of National Science Foundation Grant Number S038567 to the Research Foundation of the State University of New York. However, any opinions, findings, conclusions, or recommendations expressed herein are mine and do not necessarily reflect the views of the Foundation.

1   The Forces That Shape Instructional Materials

Instructional materials occupy the major part of a student's day. According to one estimate, 75 percent of a student's classroom time and 90 percent of homework time is spent with text materials.[1] Textbooks, workbooks, filmstrips and sound recordings compete with each other and with the teacher for student attention.

Instructional materials do not receive nearly as much attention in debates over educational policy. When they are discussed, it is usually in a negative light, as the target of complaints that they are obscene, demean minorities or are sacrilegious. Questions with positive answers are less frequently asked. How can instructional materials be made to instruct children more effectively? Why have developments in instructional materials lagged so far behind advances in medicine, agriculture and space travel? Questions are rarely asked about the underlying forces that shape instructional materials.

America's response to the Soviet Union's launching of the first successful artificial space satellite provides a dramatic example of this disregard for underlying conditions. No sooner had Sputnik been launched than policy makers instinctively turned to education as a key vehicle for securing the nation's strategic position. Because technology had historically contributed to the nation's strength in other areas, it seemed natural that it could similarly be employed to increase instructional productivity. The only question was how much research and development expenditure was needed to give education a quick technological fix. Scant attention was paid to the relations between the structure of American schools and their receptivity to innovation, or between the balance sheets of educational publishers and their capacity to develop and market instructional inventions.

In retrospect, the mistake of the early 1960s is clear. Increased research and development expenditures at one time might have made a difference, but too many stumbling blocks had accumulated by the 1960s for these expenditures to have any real effect. Local control over schooling and teacher resistance to innovation combined to blunt the effects of increased federal funding. Some schools closed their doors to the new materials. Others acquired the materials, but only to let them gather dust in storerooms. Also, university research and development workers had no integrated scientific base from which to draw, and instructional materials producers had no research and development tradition to sustain them.

The lesson of the Sputnik years, that dollars alone will not buy better instructional materials, has apparently been lost on federal policy makers in the time since. The 1970 report of a federal commission on instructional technology concluded characteristically: "A paucity of funds is a major obstacle to the introduction of instructional technology."[2] All of the commission's recommendations called for government subsidies, some for increased levels, but none for decreased levels. Absent from the commission's report was any systematic consideration of the many environmental conditions that stand in the way of change.

This book will examine the forces that shape the instructional materials used in elementary school classrooms and that, in concert, effectively discourage the production and use of innovative materials. Four topics are central:

Instructional technology Instructional technology in itself poses the fewest hurdles to innovation in instructional materials. Indeed, the technological possibilities are boundless, ranging from more effective workbooks to sophisticated programs of computer-assisted instruction. The real limitations lie not in technology, but in the behavior of consumers and producers and in the structure of federal subsidy programs.

Consumers On the consumer side of the instructional materials marketplace, traditions of uniform schools, state and local control over schooling, and formal and informal materials selection practices all contrive against receptivity to innovation.

Producers On the producer side, market structure and the failure of incentive systems to offer substantial inducements account for the low level of investment in invention.

Subsidies Subsidy programs, particularly those funded and administered by the federal government, have sought to overcome the prevailing patterns of consumer and producer resistance. The history of almost all these programs shows that they too are confined by structural limitations.

These four topics are respectively the subjects of the four chapters that follow.

The book's sixth and concluding chapter takes up the theme that increased spending alone cannot be expected to increase the efficacy of instructional materials significantly. Changes in the structure of consumption, production and subsidy must precede any such advances. The point of chapter 6, and of the book, is that the public purse is not bottomless and that, so long as these other changes are not made, the many millions of dollars now devoted to instructional materials research and development can be put to better use in equally important areas that are more effectively organized for change.

One reason that innovation in instructional materials has been so widely misunderstood is that the conditions surrounding it have been approached individually rather than as the interlocking network they actually form. Those who complain about schools' resistance to innovation wrongly assume that if schools suddenly became innovative, publishers would provide them with the innovative materials that they would then demand. Those who criticize educational publishers' conservative production decisions wrongly assume that if publishers would only provide innovative materials, the public schools would be quick to purchase them. The rest of this chapter is aimed at correcting these narrow approaches, first by summarizing the main forces at work on all sides of the instructional materials market, and then by describing the role these forces played in the history of one widely adopted instructional innovation, *Science—A Process Approach.*

Schooling, Technology, and Law

First, some truisms. The instructional materials market is made up of consumers—schools, school boards, and state agencies across the country—and of producers—well over one hundred private firms, some large, most small. The content of instructional materials is determined by producers' perceptions of what consumers will buy. These perceptions have generally led firms to produce materials much like those already on the market, and to avoid sharp departures in instructional method.

The only remarkable thing about these facts is the extent to which they have been ignored in the formation of policies aimed at increasing innovation in instructional materials. Perhaps this is because it is thought that lessons drawn from the operation of private markets are irrelevant to planning for change in instructional materials. After all, the market for instructional materials departs in many respects from the markets classically supposed by economic theory. It may seem important that the schools, school boards and state agencies that purchase instructional materials are, in a very real sense, not their consumers. Students, on whose behalf these purchasers presumably act, are the actual consumers of instructional materials. Also, these surrogate consumers do not pay for the goods they select in the sense that a household pays for the goods and services it buys. Whoever makes the purchase, it is the taxpayer who foots the bill.

Further, the federal government wields considerable influence in the instructional materials marketplace. Some publishers compete for the benefits of federal subsidies to instructional materials research and development. All feel federal pressure in less direct ways. State and local textbook purchases are frequently supported by federal grants and may as a consequence be affected by the attitudes of federal administrators. It would be interesting to discover the effects on school administrators and publishers of a plea, made by the United States Commissioner of Education during the controversy in Kanawha, West Virginia, over allegedly obscene school books, that educational publishers "print materials that do not insult the values of most parents." The Bible, McGuffy's *Readers*, and *The Wizard of Oz* were pointed to as examples of books "that present interesting stories while also teaching proper values."[3]

Yet, any differences between the market for instructional materials and the markets for other goods are differences of detail, not kind. The interests of school boards, students and taxpayers may diverge, but the tensions and balances struck between them form a single pattern of preference discernible by instructional materials producers. Producers may be attracted by offers of "free" programs developed under federal subsidy, but will weigh the benefits to be derived from this largesse against the funds that they must privately commit to the program's further development and against the risk that the end product will not meet the aggregate needs of school boards, students and taxpayers. The market for instructional materials may be crowded with public decisions, but it is a market nonetheless. It is crucial to view any prospects for change from within this perspective.

The one characteristic of this market that dominates all others is its accumulated bias against significant change in instructional materials. And the single most important factor contributing to this bias is the neighborhood school. Under the prevailing system of public education, parents may hold widely different views about schooling's proper objects, yet send their children to the same schools, to use the same instructional materials. In response, schools will pursue only the most general objectives and will acquire materials that they believe are least likely to offend the holders of any particular view. In Christopher Jencks's phrase, school systems put "a premium not on achieving a few spectacular successes but on avoiding any spectacular failures."[4] Schools select, and producers produce, materials that are not likely to upset the delicate balance already reached among contending interests. Materials that seek vigorously to advance a single educational objective are discouraged.

Nor are parents the only ones whose interests must be accommodated. Teachers also differ on instructional method. Some think that it is most important to teach subject matter content, others that it is more important for students to be exposed to the process of learning. Teachers' diverse outlooks on instructional style must be reduced to their single most acceptable common denominator when decisions are made on the production of instructional materials. Materials must be designed to accommodate those teachers who believe that they should be at the center of classroom activity and in full control, as well as those who favor a more dispersed, student-centered classroom environment.

Instructional materials are, then, shaped to accommodate the interests and potential vetoes to be exercised by education's many participants—legislators, administrators, school board members, parents, teachers, and even students. And the surest, least costly way to succeed with new materials is to follow the patterns successfully established by materials already in use.

Departures from existing patterns will occasionally be mandated, as in statutes requiring that texts adequately reflect the roles played by the nation's minority groups. And just as there are constituencies seeking fair minority representation, so doubtless there are constituencies that press for the adoption of innovative, more effective instructional materials. Yet, efforts to legislate more effective instructional materials, primarily under the name "learner verification," have proved to be toothless. And because the interests of innovative constituencies must be accommodated with those of more conservative groups, change has been reduced to its most superficial attributes, such as more colorful and stylish illustrations and typography.

Ironically, it is schools' flexibility, their capacity to accommodate many divergent interests, that is chiefly responsible for their resistance to change. The system is one of compromise, in which teachers and students are presented with instructional materials that probably few find ideal but that are least offensive to all. This may explain the teacher practice, observed in many school districts, of using photocopied or homemade instructional materials while officially adopted texts sit unopened on the classroom shelf. It may also explain the fact that in one city school observed, although there was much student vandalism and theft, there was no reported incident of a textbook being stolen.

Given the accumulated force of these and other factors, it is only partially relevant to ask, as did the title of an article describing the retreat of private firms from instructional research and development after the 1960s, "Has The Education Industry Lost Its Nerve?"[5] The "conventional view," that "education may not be ready for technology after all," may be the only view for a publisher to take if purchasers' preferences are to be met and sales maintained. Firms may be expected to engage in research and development aimed at reducing the cost of instructional materials through less expensive typesetting techniques, for example, or more efficient use of paper. However, no great hope should be placed in research and development aimed at increasing product quality through materials enabling students to learn more, and more effectively, in less time.

Research and Development

Understandably, the question might be asked, why inquire into the conditions surrounding investment in research and development? Why should special inducements be needed to attract investment to research and development, but not to other industrial activities? A producer of school desks will invest in the materials and labor needed to manufacture his product on the expectation that their cost will be returned to him by consumers paying for the product. Why can the market mechanism not similarly be relied upon to return his investment in research and development?

A modification of the school desk example will suggest the answer. Suppose that, in addition to materials and labor, the producer spent money developing a novel design for his school desk. Competitors wishing to copy the desk would be put to roughly the same expense as he for materials and labor, and would enjoy no competitive advantage over him in these respects. However, unlike the producer, these competitors would not have to pay for developing the novel design. As soon as the producer's first desk reached the market, its novel aspects would be accessible and freely replicable by all. Because competitors would enjoy free something for which the producer had been required to pay, they would enjoy a competitive advantage over him. *The critical point, of course, is that none of this—invention or imitation—will occur. Anticipating his competitors' imitations, and his own consequent inability to recover the value of his investment in the design, the manufacturer will not invest in research and development in the first place.*

This example illustrates what economists call inappropriability: because an invention is free to all once it is communicated, its value cannot be appropriated by its developer. This phenomenon explains the unwillingness of private firms, absent special inducement, to invest in the research and development required to produce invention. It also indicates the role of mechanisms such as copyright and patent law, intended to reduce inappropriability by securing to the developer a period of limited monopoly during which he can recover his investment.

The research and development picture is in practice not nearly so stark. The producer may attempt to dissuade his customers from dealing with competitors by appealing to their moral sense with the argument that he was first with the invention. Priority will also give the producer the advantage of lead time over his competitors. While competitors are retooling to incorporate his advance in their products, he can reap the benefits of initial sales and possibly generate brand loyalty as well. Yet, as will be seen, the conditions surrounding instructional materials purchase offer little room for moral claims or the advantages of lead time.

Where invention lies not in a product but in its method of manufacture, the producer can appropriate part of the invention's value by sequestering the vital information within his plant. But this prospect provides little solace to the producer of instructional materials, in which inventive elements will typically be revealed on the face of the product. And even appropriation through secrecy will be incomplete. Trusted, knowledgeable employees defect to the ranks of competitors with irritating frequency. Piracy aside, competitors can often determine from an analysis of the inventor's product the means employed in its manufacture.

Finally, firms will generally be more likely to invest in applied research, which leads to incremental advances, than in basic research capable of yielding larger, more significant advances. Inappropriability is the principal source of this bias, for basic research generates external benefits to a far greater extent than does applied research, the results of which can be incorporated more fully into the inventor's products. The implication of this phenomenon for instructional materials is to reduce the already sparse incentives to invest in the development of major inventions.

The Role of Law

Law has a varied impact on innovation in instructional materials. The patent and copyright laws are the chief mechanisms available to attract private investment to instructional materials research and development. Granting property protection to the fruits of research and development, and thus enabling the entrepreneur to bar their unauthorized use by competitors, the patent and copyright laws can attract investment to what would otherwise be largely unrewarded efforts.

Yet the coverage of the copyright and patent laws is not complete, and large bodies of subject matter and research and development effort go unprotected. The copyright law protects expressions but not ideas. Patent law refuses protection to natural principles and basic scientific truths. As a consequence, neither body of law offers any real incentive to the development of new, fundamental techniques to be incorporated in instructional materials.

Even if patent and copyright law did protect investments of this order, it is doubtful that significantly innovative instructional products would result. It is one thing to create mechanisms for appropriating an invention's value and quite another to create a market for the invented products. Schools are overwhelmingly conservative in their selection of instructional materials, preferring already tried products to dramatic departures. Facing this resistance to change, producers have no motive to invest in research and development aimed at significantly innovative instructional materials. The patent and copyright laws may be used to attract investment to the production of invention, but there are no comparable mechanisms to induce schools to invest in the consumption of invention.

At the heart of the problem is the principle embodied in the constitutions of many states, and in the traditions of others, that the state's public school system be uniform. Indiana's constitutional provision is typical: "Knowledge and learning, generally diffused throughout a community, being essential to the preservation of a free government; it shall be the duty of the General Assembly to encourage by all suitable means, moral, intellectual, scientific, and agricultural improvement; *and to provide by law, for a general and uniform system of common schools*, wherein tuition shall be without charge."[6]

In a recent decision examining a similar constitutional provision, the Washington Supreme Court characterized a "general and uniform system" as "one in which every child in the state has free access to certain minimum and reasonably standardized educational and instructional facilities and opportunities through at least the 12th grade." A uniform system should, in the court's view, be "administered with that degree of uniformity which enables a child to transfer from one district to another within the same grade without substantial loss of credit or standing and with access by each student of whatever grade to acquire those skills and training that are reasonably understood to be fundamental and basic to a sound education."[7]

Of itself, uniformity does not necessarily imply resistance to innovation, for a state's schools could be directed as uniformly toward change as away from it. Rather, resistance stems from the fact that if only one form of public school and one main curriculum can exist within a state, the varied interests of all parents, teachers and administrators must be accommodated to that single form. Only if state systems were diverse would these accommodations be unnecessary. And only with diversity would there be diverse markets for instructional materials. Some schools would seek materials like those that have always been used. Other schools, interested in experimenting with new directions in instructional method, would seek more innovative materials.

While traditions of school uniformity remain steadfast, the law has been moving away from the requirement that textbooks also be uniform. An increasing number of states are shifting from an "adoption" position, in which major responsibility for selecting materials is lodged in the state government, to a "nonadoption" position, in which the bulk of authority is vested in largely autonomous school districts. Further, widening legal concepts of academic freedom will in many situations enable teachers to substitute their own choices for the materials officially selected. An 1899 case, in which a public school teacher was fined ten dollars for violating his state's Uniform Textbook Act by using a geography text that had not been adopted by the state textbook commission, truly belongs more to the nineteenth than to the twentieth century.[8]

Moves to decentralize the text selection process might appear to promise a new diversity in instructional materials. It seems more likely, however, that, at least so far as innovative materials are concerned, earlier conditions will persist. Almost all of the contending forces affecting text selection decisions at the state level are present at the local level as well, requiring the same degrees of compromise on instructional materials' content and method. And while these compromises might variously be tinged by local concerns, the differences are probably both too subtle and too specific to be accounted for in the investment decisions of the nation's instructional materials producers. The paradox of local control is that it leads to national uniformity in instructional materials' method and content.

Efforts to reverse the prevailing patterns of resistance to innovation in instructional materials through the judicial process also seem doomed to failure. Courts typically reject parental, and even teacher, requests to review official decisions on materials and curriculum. The reason usually given is that it is not the place of the judiciary to second guess the discretionary exercises of school administrators.

On those rare occasions when courts have been persuaded to intervene in school decisions, the result has generally been to expand rather than to narrow the number of contending interests that must be accommodated within a single school, so that instructional materials must be designed to achieve a still broader compromise. For example, *Brown v. Board of Education*,[9] the United States Supreme Court's landmark desegregation decision, enlarged the range of interests and objectives to be served by the neighborhood school. And busing to achieve racial balance, though it may have weakened the concept of the neighborhood school, has done nothing to align individual schools with diverse methodological outlooks. Indeed, diversity might be condemned for covertly reintroducing systems of schools that are "separate but equal." *Brown* and its progeny may significantly hamper future efforts to differentiate schools, whether through voucher or other systems.

A lawsuit begun 5 November 1975, in the United States District Court for the Northern District of Mississippi, illustrates the constitutional trend toward comprehensiveness. The complaint, filed by students, teachers, school officials and leaders of the Catholic and Episcopal dioceses, charged that defendants, the Mississippi History Textbook Committee and the Mississippi State Purchasing Board, had wrongfully excluded a revisionist state history, *Mississippi: Conflict and Change*, from its approved textbook list. (Under the text selection procedures followed in Mississippi at the time, school boards would be reimbursed by the state only for purchases of materials included on the approved list.)

Plaintiffs sought not to displace the text in use, *Mississippi: Yesterday and Today*, but only to have their preferred text listed along with it. Asserting that, historically, the Textbook Rating Committee and its predecessors "have adopted for use in all history courses taught in Mississippi, only those texts which minimize, ignore or denigrate the role of blacks and other minorities," the complaint argued that the existing process of selecting textbooks violated the due process and equal protection clauses of the Fourteenth Amendment, denying children the right to a fully nondiscriminatory public school system.[10]

If the lawsuit is successful, Mississippi's schools will be in a position to choose between two different history texts. If the texts differ sharply, parents may be expected to clash over which of the two will be adopted in their district. Such clashes, or the fear of them, will over the long run lead to texts that diverge less dramatically. If *Mississippi: Conflict and Change* enjoys a substantial number of adoptions, the publishers of *Mississippi: Yesterday and Today* can be expected to go after the lost markets by incorporating many of the milder revisionist points in their own next edition.

In the end, the result achieved through autonomous district choice will probably be no different than if the Mississippi legislature, like some other state legislatures, had specifically required that all history texts used in the state give a balanced portrayal of minority contributions. The same kind of compromise, whether at the local or state level, can be expected when innovative instructional techniques are at issue.

One Idea That "Worked"

Of all the instructional programs introduced into the elementary grades in recent decades, probably none has won more widespread or lasting acceptance than *Science–A Process Approach (S-APA)*. A brief review of the program's origins, content and eventual dissemination will highlight some of the prospects and pitfalls that lie before instructional materials research and development generally.[11]

Funded by the National Science Foundation, developed by the American Association for the Advancement of Science and marketed by the Xerox Education Division, *S-APA* is a complete general science program for kindergarten through sixth grade. The program focuses on scientific processes such as observing, classifying, interpreting data and experimenting. The program places little emphasis on reading skills, and early evaluations show student achievement to be largely unaffected by economic, ethnic, educational, social or geographic factors.

Initiating the Product

The origins of *S-APA* lie in three regional conferences conducted by the American Association for the Advancement of Science (AAAS) to help the National Science Foundation (NSF) determine whether the foundation should become involved in supporting elementary school science programs. The conferences, attended by teachers, school administrators, science educators, scientists and psychologists, focused on two questions: Would scientists be interested in working on curriculum programs for the elementary level? Did teachers at this level feel a need for new programs? Answering both questions affirmatively and citing an urgent need for improved science instruction in the elementary grades, the conferences proposed that a major curriculum effort be undertaken.

Specifically, the conference recommended that schools be given an array of several science programs from which to choose. Following this recommendation, NSF decided to fund five elementary level science curriculum development projects. One of these was *S-APA*, and it was to be developed by AAAS through its Commission on Science Education. From spring 1962 through September 1969 NSF spent approximately $2,250,000 on the development of *S-APA*.

The Commission on Science Education was evidently attracted to the conference recommendations that science instruction be interdisciplinary, that it stress the spirit of discovery, that it be presented in a progressive sequence of instruction, and that teacher training be integrated into the program. The commission also adopted the proposal that scientists, classroom teachers, administrators, science educators and educational psychologists all be involved in the preparation of program materials.

Two eight-day planning conferences held in summer 1962 gave more specific direction to the project and gave the commission a basis for devising a general development plan. As it evolved in practice, the plan contemplated an annual cycle of activity. Winter and spring were for the commission staff to organize the development activities that would occupy the remainder of the year. Summer was for writing sessions involving teachers, school administrators, psychologists, and scientists from relevant disciplines. Fall was for the commission staff to edit, compile and produce the materials and distribute them to school try-out centers throughout the country. During the school year, teachers at the try-out centers would report their experience with the program, following forms and procedures provided by the commission. This information would then be used in revising the materials during the next summer writing session.

Each of the five summer writing sessions typically involved thirty-five to fifty participants and lasted from six to eight weeks. Participants were organized into committees to write new exercises and to work with laboratory personnel in identifying and designing equipment for the activities. In revising earlier exercises, the committees relied not only on the evaluations provided by teachers at try-out centers but also on student performance on specified objectives. The goal was that 90 percent of the students achieve 90 percent of the objectives. In each of the five years of development, from eleven to fourteen try-out centers were used, with between forty-eight and 242 teachers involved in any one year.

The Product

S-APA rests on the theory that learning can be broken down into component skills and that these skills are most effectively arranged and taught in hierarchical order, from simple to complex. It is these hierarchies that form the continuing structure of *S-APA*. The marriage of theory to curriculum was described by Robert Gagne, a principal architect of *S-APA*: "One can construct a reasonable sequence of instruction which aims to have children acquire process skills, beginning with simple kinds of observation, and building progressively through classifying, measuring, communicating, quantifying, organizing through space and time, to the making of inferences and prediction. As further building occurs, one finds it possible for students to learn how to make operational definitions, how to formulate testable hypotheses, how to carry out experiments and how to interpret data from experiments."[12]

Another theoretical underpinning of *S-APA* was elsewhere said by Gagne to imply that "learning will be most effective when relationships are 'discovered' [by the student] rather than 'copied,' when generalizations are attained rather than being imposed."[13] Any conflict between the straitjacket implied by hierarchies and the freedom implied by discovery was resolved in favor of the hierarchical approach. The overriding conviction appears to be that discovery will be most effective when it is induced along specified, well-tried paths.

The first edition of *S-APA* was divided into seven parts, with each part normally taught at successive grade levels, K through 6. Each part was divided into between twenty and twenty-five sequenced exercises, and each exercise was intended to teach one or more behaviors. One change made in the second edition was to drop the division of exercises by grade, so that a teacher will not feel compelled to complete in any year a designated number of exercises—or "modules" as they are called in the second edition.

Typically, the teacher introduces each *S-APA* exercise by demonstrating the materials to be used in it and asking questions about them. The main part of the lesson consists of one or more prescribed activities, followed by "generalizing experiences," in which the students seek to apply what they have learned in the activities. This is followed by evaluation of student performance. The program occupies about twenty-five minutes a day in kindergarten and about forty-five minutes in the higher grades.

A booklet designed for each exercise informs the teacher about the behavioral objectives of the exercise, the place and relative importance of the exercise in the overall program hierarchy, and new vocabulary and materials needed by the students to perform the exercise. The booklet guides the "generalizing experience," in which students relate what they have learned in the exercise to a new situation in a different context, and provides for an "appraisal" to evaluate overall class performance, and a "competency measure" that can be administered individually as a more focused measure of student achievement.

The method of *S-APA* implies not only that student behavior will be closely directed by the classroom teacher, but also that teacher behavior will be closely controlled by procedures set out in the curriculum. Instructional procedures described in the booklet include the required and optional activities for the exercise and suggest how the activities should be introduced. The following instructions[14] are typical:

Activity 1
Let the children watch as you fill a plastic test tube with cool water and put in several drops of food coloring so that the water is easier to see. Insert a piece of stiff plastic tubing about 25 centimeters long (lubricated with oil, grease, or

soap) into a wet one-hole stopper, and put the stopper far enough into the opening of the test tube so that the liquid rises to a height of several centimeters in the tubing. Do not trap any air beneath the stopper. Attach a card to the tube with plastic tape so that the liquid level and the symbols you will add during the course of the activity are easy to see, as in Figure 1. Then use a crayon or felt marking pen to indicate the liquid level in the tube at room temperature (R).

Now close one hand around the test tube to warm it. Let the children watch the level of the colored fluid rise in the tubing as the test tube becomes warmer, and mark the water level B.

Ask, "What is happening?" (The liquid is rising in the tubing.)

"Why is it going up? Have we added any water?" (No.) If the children say that you are pressing it up or that pressure is forcing the fluid up, have a child lift the test tube gently from your hand to prove that you are not holding it tightly. Again ask why the fluid is going up. The children will probably suggest that the rise of the fluid may be due to the warmth of your hand. "What is this called? Does anyone know the word *expansion*? When a volume gets larger, it is expanding. What is a volume doing when it gets smaller?" (Contracting.)

Ask, "How can you find out whether it is really the warmth of my hand that is causing the rise?" The children may suggest any of the following:

1. Set the test tube down and see whether the fluid falls in the tube (to R).
2. Put the test tube into hot water to see whether the liquid in the tube rises or falls.
3. Put the test tube into ice water to see whether the liquid in the tube rises or falls.
4. Let someone else hold the test tube.

At this point, let different groups of children try each of these suggestions, with the rest of the class watching. When they try Suggestion 2, mark the high point that the water reaches with an H (hot); and for Suggestion 3, mark the low point C (cold). When each trial is completed, ask a member of the group to summarize the result for the class. The children should see that there is a relationship between the change of temperature and the change in the level of the fluid in the tube.

Divide the children into groups of three or four. Tell each group to make its own thermometer using water and food coloring. If they work on cafeteria trays, it will be easier to clean up any spilled water. It would also be a good idea to insert the tubing into the stoppers yourself to avoid broken tubing and cut hands.

When the children have finished making their thermometers, have them mark them with crayon to show the fluid levels at the temperature of the room and in a mixture of ice and water. Discuss the advantage of using these thermometers instead of just feeling whether something is warm, hot, or very hot. "How can you tell by using the thermometer if two glasses of water are at the same temperature?" (The fluid in the tube rises to the same level when the thermometer is placed in each glass.) "How can you keep a record of how hot something is?" (By marking the level the fluid reaches in the tube.)

Process Development Laboratories "containing equipment and supplies for a class of thirty children" represent the basic materials for each of the curriculum's seven parts. In addition to exercise booklets, and a self-instruction manual,

Commentary for Teachers, the first edition provided teachers with hierarchy charts outlining the development of process skills throughout the program. The second edition replaces the hierarchy chart with a "planning chart," ostensibly aimed at increasing the program's flexibility. There are few printed materials for the students.

A sampling of the focus and materials for the first grade, Part B, will give some idea of the program's approach and the kinds of materials it employs. Kindergarten, Part A, introduced students to observing differences and similarities in objects. Part B built on this by introducing students to change and comparison. Among the exercises in Part B were linear measurement, variation in objects of the same kind, observing color and color changes in plants, seeds and seed germination. This part in turn set the stage for the second grade, Part C, which extended observation exercises to communicating observations, inferring and predicting.

Generally, the items supplied with the Standard Kit for Part B were of a sort that would be inconvenient for the individual teacher to obtain on his own. They included: one paper isosceles triangle and one balloon for each child; thirty thermometers with the Celsius scale; ten weather charts on which to record daily observations, two cylinders and two cones with open bases, each having the same base area and the same altitude; six bar magnets (not marked N and S); six bars, the same shape as the magnets but not magnets; red and blue paper; mung bean seeds; and graph paper.

Items needed for Part B, but not included in the kit, were generally easy to obtain or perishable. Among them were: a toy turtle (plastic or wood); a live turtle; popcorn and equipment for popping it; a marshmallow for each child; several potatoes of the same variety, but differing in size, shape, color and skin texture; white vinegar; flower buds which are beginning to open; one clam (if available). Many of these items (but presumably not the clam) were supplied with the more expensive Comprehensive Kit.

According to a November 1970 price list, the price of a Standard Kit for Part B, designed for thirty students, and delivered in corrugated cardboard storage modules, was $217. The price of the Comprehensive Kit was $280. For Standard and Comprehensive sets of expendable materials for Part B, the charges were thirty dollars and fifty-eight dollars respectively. The price of the Hierarchy Chart for grades K-3 was $6.00 and for grades 4-6 was $10.50. The *Commentary for Teachers* sold for $7.

Disseminating the Product

Efforts to disseminate *S-APA* were well attuned to the special characteristics of the instructional materials market. It was recognized that private firms are the institutions primarily responsible for production and marketing, and it early became clear that if *S-APA* was to compete successfully in the marketplace, these responsibilities could not be retained by AAAS, but rather would have to be transferred to a private entrepreneur. It was also recognized that classroom teachers substantially influence decisions to purchase and use instructional materials. If this new program was to succeed, teachers would have to be trained in its use and convinced that the program was an aid, not a threat, to their classroom role. AAAS met the first need through an agreement with Xerox Corporation to publish and market the materials. It met the second through ambitious programs of teacher training and public relations.

The selection of Xerox as publisher of *S-APA* was made in 1966, four years after program development had begun, and a publication contract was executed in 1967. Under terms set down by the National Science Foundation, the claimed copyright in the work was to be limited to five years from the date of publication by Xerox, effectively fifty-one years short of the period of protection then possible under the copyright law. Xerox was also to pay a six percent royalty to AAAS to be forwarded to the United States Treasury. General policy decisions affecting the program were to be made by an advisory council consisting of two voting members each from AAAS and Xerox, a nonvoting chairman from AAAS, and a nonvoting secretary from Xerox. However, the final word on program content was to rest with AAAS, and on pricing and sales practices with Xerox.

Xerox's promotion of *S-APA* since publication of the first three parts in 1967 has doubtless been aided by the efforts of AAAS and others dating back to the program's inception in 1962. The involvement of influential science educators from the very first conferences, the experimental try-out program in schools throughout the country, speeches, presentations and demonstration films all certainly helped to create a market for the program. A newsletter published regularly by the Commission on Science Education reported early developments in the program, including test results from try-out centers, and in later years announced training programs and the publication of new literature about the program. A *Commentary for Teachers* explaining the program was prepared, as was a *Guide for Inservice Instruction* designed for use in teacher training.

The process approach generally, and use of *S-APA* specifically, have become prominent objects in the continuing education offerings of universities and teacher education institutions. The announcement of a 1971 workshop at the University of Georgia is typical:

Workshop on Science—A Process Approach; June 14–July 2; for elementary school personnel and those engaged in teacher preparation at the college level. During the workshop the participants will examine and manipulate the equipment, review the philosophy, rationale and printed materials, and use the study in a micro-teaching situation. The workshop will meet from 8 a.m. till 12 noon, Monday through Friday, for three weeks. Five quarter hours of undergraduate or graduate credit will be offered for those completing the workshop. . . .

Many institutions have introduced the process approach into their regular curriculum and instruction courses.

The Eastern Regional Institute for Education (ERIE), one of a national network of federally funded laboratories aimed at bridging the gap between instructional theory and practice, also became involved in dissemination of *S-APA*. The ERIE project had two main objects. The first was to install *S-APA* in diverse schools throughout the laboratory's region, encompassing northern and western Pennsylvania and all of New York except New York City. The second object was to monitor the installation, to test and improve the installation and monitoring system, and to make the system available for replication by others.[15]

During the 1967–68 and 1968–69 school years, ERIE provided a comprehensive range of materials and support services to twenty-one pilot schools. Materials included teacher manuals, kits of materials and replacement supplies. Services included preliminary conferences and week-long summer workshops for teachers and administrators, biweekly or triweekly consultant visits by ERIE staff associates and, when requested, training of local "process leaders." A petty cash fund was also provided to enable the immediate local purchase of incidental materials. The intent of the project was for ERIE gradually to withdraw its support and for the pilot schools to assume full responsibility for the installed curriculum.

Having successfully paved the way for *S-APA*, these dissemination efforts also opened a path for imitators. On 6 March 1972, Xerox and AAAS filed a complaint against Sigma Scientific, Inc., charging it with copyright and trademark infringement and unfair competition. Sigma answered that it had, since 1969, packaged kits of supplies and equipment for use in *S-APA* exercises and that it offered these materials for sale at prices substantially below those charged by Xerox. Sigma also asserted that it did not sell the printed exercise manuals and that, in fact, it advised its customers that the necessary manuals had to be separately purchased from Xerox. Because of its customers' difficulties in obtaining these manuals, Sigma said, it sought unsuccessfully to purchase the manuals directly from Xerox. According to Sigma, it "was advised by Xerox that no manuals would be sold to Sigma and that it was the 'policy' of Xerox to sell the Program Manuals 'only to the direct users of the program which are educational institutions.'"[16]

The action against Sigma was later stayed. While the truth of Xerox's allegations and Sigma's cross-allegations may thus never be known, the controversy does illumine the nature of Xerox's dilemma. Its relatively common program supplies and equipment were not protected or protectable by copyright or patent, and could freely be copied by others. Also, the materials published by Xerox had to meet high quality standards set by AAAS and could easily be underpriced by the less deluxe versions produced by competitors.

Further, although the printed materials in the program were protected by copyright, the shelter afforded was not particularly commodious. Under copyright law, competitors can be enjoined from copying a copyright proprietor's protected expression but are free to appropriate the expression's underlying ideas, method and structure. This meant that competitors of Xerox could emulate the basic structure and technique of *S-APA*, and by recasting the instructions in their own words, could escape copyright liability. And, apart from this sort of behavior by competitors, many teachers in a school or school system could share a single booklet. Doubtless, materials were often photocopied illicitly or under cover of copyright's fair-use doctrine, which excuses certain acts of copyright infringement when done for educational purposes. In short, Xerox was faced with the reality that a hard-pressed school system need only buy—or borrow—one Xerox kit to go into business as a publisher itself, photocopying the printed materials and purchasing equipment and supplies from cutrate competitors.

The Conditions for Change

S-APA worked. It achieved widespread acceptance in the nation's schools, satisfied its sponsors, probably earned a profit for its publisher, and produced some measurable gains in student achievement. Yet to say that the program worked is not to say that it led every student to knowledge and insights more valuable than those each could otherwise have acquired in the time spent with the program. Brief reflection on the nature of the product, the behavior of its consumers and its producer and the impact of the subsidies that supported it will begin to suggest how altered conditions might have produced instructional materials more closely approaching an optimum of student productivity.

The Product. *S-APA* embodies objectives followed by many other contemporary programs for increasing instructional efficiency. It is premised on the inquiry method, an approach to learning that has won wide support at least since the time of John Dewey. Its orientation is strongly technological, in that it calls for rigid and repeated adherence to a series of prescribed steps, contemplating certain results. It also employs evaluative procedures intended to measure the extent to which classroom pursuit of steps and method produces the anticipated results.

At the same time, *S-APA* is not an instructional product in the conventional sense. Unlike the variety of texts, games or workbooks that are available to teachers and children and that can be used at the students' own pace, *S-APA* is exclusively designed for use by teachers, its lessons and procedures to be communicated by them to an entire classroom of students. Thus, while *S-APA* may increase instructional efficiency by incorporating a well-tried instructional approach in a rigidly structured, constantly repeated and evaluated program, it falls short of the optimum in not also enabling individualized instruction. Part of the reason for this can be traced to the habits of consumers and to the incentives available to producers.

Consumers. Among the recommendations produced by the regional conferences that preceded the National Science Foundation's decision to fund *S-APA* was one that the preparation of materials should involve not only scientists, science educators and educational psychologists, but also classroom teachers and administrators. Teachers, more than any other individuals in the schooling enterprise, influence the selection of instructional materials, and the success of *S-APA* can in large part be attributed to its extensive accommodation of teacher interests. Consultant visits, training programs and courses for credit went part of the way to make this accommodation. Probably more significant was the fact that, by centering all its procedures on the teacher, the program in no way threatened the teacher's classroom position. Indeed, it did much to consolidate the teacher's classroom control. The question remains, though, whether the price paid for accommodating teacher needs was reduced fulfillment of students' needs.

The Producer. The role of Xerox in the development of *S-APA* consisted of refining the materials produced by AAAS's summer workshops and promoting and distributing the finished product. It would be interesting to see the program that it might have produced had it been offered different incentives. For example, the firm's copyright in elements of the program was limited to five years. Would it have invested more or differently in the program's development if a full twenty-eight year term were offered with a renewal option of another twenty-eight years? What would have been the countervailing costs to competitors and consumers if a full copyright term had been offered?

Many elements in the program were too old or too common to be protected by copyright or patent, which require originality and novelty. Would protection of these elements under some other system have altered Xerox's investment toward any more desirable directions? Other elements important to the program, mainly its underlying scientific precepts, are unprotectable because they are thought to be too important to be privately monopolized through mechanisms such as copyright or patent. Would the promise of protection for basic scientific discoveries offer an inducement to firms like Xerox to invest in the research needed to produce these discoveries? Would the resulting patterns of private investment be more desirable than the patterns presently produced by investments like those made by the National Science Foundation?

Subsidies. In theory, subsidy programs need suffer none of the limitations encountered among producers and consumers. Those who give subsidies require no promise of profit to invest in the production or adoption of innovation. Yet, if not concerned with profits, those who administer these programs are presumably interested in their success and will make their investments accordingly. The AAAS Commission on Science Education clearly kept teacher receptivity to *S-APA* as a prominent, if implicit, objective in the program's design. The National Science Foundation is particularly sensitive to congressional charges that the foundation's more dramatic educational programs have improperly intruded a federal presence into public schooling, historically a state and local domain. It would be interesting to discover the extent to which the initial conception of *S-APA* was tempered by anxieties over local resistance.

Products, consumers, producers, and subsidies together form the market for instructional materials. They, and the market, are shaped by a tangled net of public decisions—statutes, regulations and administrative behavior. Each of the chapters that follow examines one of these elements, its surrounding environment of public decisions and their implications for the level and direction of investment in instructional materials research and development. A final chapter describes the kinds of environmental changes that will be required for modest and for dramatic advances to be made in instructional materials.

2 Instructional Technology: Past, Present, and Future

Instructional technology is popularly associated with machines—glittering consoles, fabulous instrument panels and the hum of meshing gears. The image has been perpetuated by both supporters and detractors of instructional technology. Mechanization, according to the supporters, is technology's key to systematized and more efficient instruction. Mechanization and technology, say the opponents, will reduce students to robots, making education less humane.

In fact, instructional technology is defined neither by machines nor by automation. Technology simply makes routine the steps necessary to achieve a desired object. It is a formula or recipe which specifies the materials, labor, and timing needed to attain a given result. To be sure, these elements may be mechanically combined, as in programs of computer-assisted instruction in which students and a computer interact over a console displaying carefully patterned materials. Yet technology may also be embodied in texts or workbooks which provide the same predetermined information to student after student. Or, as in *Science—A Process Approach*, technology may involve no more than a teacher's following prescribed steps in instructing students.

Programmed instruction suggests some aspects of instructional technology's larger possibilities. In programmed instruction, materials are aimed at systematically achieving a desired learning goal. Commonly, a program prescribes several interrelated steps for the student to follow in an ordered sequence. The student's success at each step signals his or her ability to move on to the next step. A program may combine hardware and software, as in teaching machines and computer-assisted instruction, or it may employ books alone. A well-known example is the workbook that leads the student from question to question along a path of increasing difficulty until the end objective is obtained. A key educational benefit of programmed instruction is that it enables differentiation among students according to ability, with faster learners proceeding more rapidly through increasingly difficult materials.

In approaching the larger prospects for programmed instruction and for instructional materials generally, care must be taken to distinguish between the forms or media in which instructional materials are packaged and the content of these packages. There has been far more innovation in instructional media than in the instructional messages they contain. Opaque projectors and film strips represent advances over blackboards, maps and charts, but their innovations lie in techniques of demonstration, not learning. Videotapes serve all the functions of sound-synchronized film, but will not begin to make a distinctive educational

21

contribution until their special capabilities are applied to qualitatively different ends. What innovations have occurred in instructional hardware, and in what ways have they outstripped advances in instructional techniques? What efforts have been made at innovation in instructional techniques? The discussion that follows attempts some answers.

Hardware: Instructional Packages

Over the last fifty years films, filmstrips, audiotapes and videotapes have joined textbooks as vehicles for elementary instruction. Yet instructional content and method has remained largely the same. Why? One reason is that advances in educational hardware are byproducts of innovation in consumer goods, such as movie projectors and audio equipment, and in equipment developed for the military. Although hardware innovation, particularly by the military, was accompanied by innovations in instructional technique, these advances were not nearly as dramatic nor as readily welcomed into the educational community.

Textbooks

Of all forms of instructional materials, the textbook predominates, both historically and in the scale of its present use. The modern textbook has its origins in the colonial hornbook, the battledore, and the primer. Noah Webster's *Grammatical Institute of the English Language, Part 3*, published in 1785, was the first distinctively American school reader. The most successful reader was McGuffey's, first published in 1856, which went through seven publishing firms and even more editions, and had by 1920 reportedly accumulated sales of 122 million copies. The commercial success of the McGuffey *Reader* can be traced to its publisher's effective marketing and painstaking revisions to fit the text to the interests of a large body of teachers and school systems. In any event, McGuffey's success cannot be attributed to substantive innovation. Neither its format nor its content ever broke from the traditions established by other readers. Indeed, early McGuffey editions were plagued by competitors' cries of plagiarism and by at least one reported action for copyright infringement.[1]

Accuracy, clarity and an aversion to idiosyncracy also mark the production of modern textbooks. Because it is essentially an exposition of accepted fact and principle, the textbook generally receives intensive and widespread editorial attention. At least two copy editors will work on a text. One editor is expected to have competence in the subject matter covered—math or social studies, say. The other is expected to have competence in the grade level—elementary or high school. Many other editors will also typically be involved between the text's initial conception and its completion.

Between 1960 and 1971, publisher sales of textbooks for use in the elementary grades more than doubled, from $148.4 million in 1960 to $314 million in 1971. The growth rate in these years was fairly consistent, with some exceptions. A sharp increase of $54 million in 1966 was followed by a $14.3 million decline in 1967. At the same time, sales to elementary schools diminished as a fraction of all textbook sales, from 44 percent at the beginning of the period to 35.8 percent at its close.[2]

Audiovisual Materials

Unlike textbooks, which reflect three hundred years of evolving accommodation to school needs, most audiovisual devices belong to this century and first emerged in settings other than public schools, such as the leisure, entertainment, and defense industries. Research mounted in connection with American war efforts accelerated advances in film technology. By 1926, 16mm film and equipment for educational use was generally accessible, and by the 1930's 16mm film with synchronized sound became available. The first large-scale instructional application of audiovisual materials and techniques occurred in the military and in industry during World War II, and only subsequently in the public schools. When renewed concern for national security prompted the passage of the 1958 National Defense Education Act, funds for the purchase of audiovisual equipment and materials increased dramatically.

Slate blackboards and, to a lesser extent, large format maps and charts, are the traditional visual aids to instruction. They were joined but not displaced by lantern slides and, later, film strips. Motion pictures, particularly with synchronized sound tracks, have emerged as the mainstay of school visual aids and have enjoyed increasing economies in size and ease of use. The original 35mm reels were replaced by 16mm, and then by 8mm reels. Reels were increasingly replaced by cartridges. The chief value of the cartridge is that, by making the projector simple enough for a four- or five-year-old student to operate, it opens up new possibilities for individualized instruction through use of short—four- to ten-minute—film loops. Because it is reusable and relatively inexpensive, videotape may eventually replace film as an audiovisual medium. Furthermore, videotape offers special advantages in situations where instruction will be aided by the recording and immediate playback of a student's responses and behavior.

Developments in sound recording have had an important impact on the teaching of foreign languages in the language laboratory, where individualized instruction is a central goal. Language laboratories range in sophistication from a number of tape recorders equipped with headphones, to integrated systems with recording and monitoring consoles for teachers, tape libraries, and auxiliary facilities for film videotape viewing. Several students can simultaneously receive interactive drills in both comprehension and speaking, each student at his or her own pace. The rapid development and widespread implementation of these laboratories can in large part be attributed to generous, specially designated funding under the National Defense Education Act.

The one field in which public school adoption of new audiovisual media has fallen far short of expectations is broadcasting, both radio and television. In retrospect, the reasons are obvious. The economies of broadcasting involve service to a large audience with scheduling determined by the network or station—circumstances largely inconsistent with the school setting. In the school, the individual classroom forms the relevant audience, requiring that programming be accommodated to its autonomous schedule. Sound recordings and tapes have consequently proved more attractive than radio, and videotapes and cassettes more attractive than broadcast television, because they can be broadly distributed, stored in easily accessible central repositories, and used by the teacher or student according to his or her individual schedule.

Between 1966 and 1972 total sales of audiovisual materials to educational institutions at all levels increased from $118 to $214.7 million. Their share of the total instructional materials market grew from 14.2 percent at the beginning of the period to 19.7 percent at its close. Textbooks' share of the market declined over the same period from 85.8 percent to 80.3 percent. Between 1968 and 1972, audio-coordinated filmstrips enjoyed the most dramatic rate of growth, 305.8 percent, increasing their market share from 7.6 to 19.6 percent. Prerecorded tapes ranked second, with a growth rate of 207.4 percent and a market share increase from 5.0 percent to 9.7 percent. Silent filmstrips experienced a 25 percent decline in growth rate over the same period, second only to 16mm black and white film (28.3 percent decline), which was rapidly being displaced by 8mm silent and 16mm color films.[3]

Teaching Machines and Computer-Assisted Instruction

Programs of computer-assisted instruction, the modern successor to teaching machines, contain the most dramatic promise for tailoring instructional processes to the needs of individual students. At present, these technological possibilities are far from being realized. Teaching machines fell out of favor after a brief period of active marketing and high hopes for their contribution to instruction; and it is painfully clear that the computer's full contribution to instructional technology lies far in the future.

Teaching machines have a long history, dating at least to Halcyon Skinner's 1866 spelling machine. By the 1920s, with the introduction of the Pressey device, the basic function of the teaching machine became clear: to test the student by exposing him or her to a series of questions, and to teach the student by informing him or her immediately whether the responses to the questions were correct. In its early years, the teaching machine played only a limited role—in testing—in the otherwise nonautomated instructional enterprise. The more comprehensive instructional possibilities of teaching machines became evident in subsequent programs to instruct soldiers in the operation, assembly and disassembly of military equipment. The equipment—a gun, say—served as the machine, and the printed instructions as the program. All the necessary steps could be learned through practice, without the intervention of a teacher. The next advance, perfected by B.F. Skinner, retained the feature of comprehensiveness, but separated the content of the instructional program from the machine and applied the program to instruction in other than manual skills. This concept resulted in "an instructional mechanism used to produce systematic behavioral changes in a student whose responses to the material presented determine the further operation of the mechanism."[4]

After an initial burst of activity between 1959 and 1962, producers' interest in teaching machines declined sharply, after the market they had hoped for failed to develop. Several causes underlie the failure. First, there were deficiencies in the hardware. Most of the machines on the market were apparently designed poorly and produced hastily, with only limited appreciation of the needs of classroom use. Larger problems lay in the available software. There were insufficient programs to make investment in the machines worthwhile, and this dilemma was aggravated by the fact that programs made for one type of machine often could not be used with others. Finally, research during this initial period generally demonstrated that machines were no more effective than far less costly text and workbook programs and, indeed, that the programmed text often worked better than the machine.[5]

The prospective advantages of computer-assisted instruction over teaching machines lie only in part in increased hardware sophistication. The more substantial advantages, not yet realized, lie in increased software capabilities. Computer programs possess at least two special attributes: they can adjust the rate and order at which instructions are given to individual student needs, and they can permit branching, facilitating alternative patterns of program response determined by the nature of the student response. Software capabilities should not, however, be exaggerated. The range of branching is naturally limited by the number and range of possible student responses that the programmer is able to anticipate. More serious difficulties have been encountered in the present inability of programs to comprehend conceptually focused questions.

In a typical system under the current state of the art, a lesson might be initiated by the student's typing in his name at the console. The computer, retrieving from memory the student's performance at a given point in the course, picks up the lesson at the appropriate point, possibly checking the student's recollection of the material with two or three review questions. The pace at which materials and questions are presented to the student will increase or slacken, depending on the student's demonstrated proficiency. Indications of proficiency may also trigger omission of some presentations and speedier progress to more difficult ones. For the student who encounters difficulty with a subject, instruction may be branched, presenting a more rudimentary or differently oriented approach to the subject, with different branches followed until the student is prepared to return to the main track.

As it is now conceived, computer-assisted instruction enables drill, tutorial and dialogue exercises in the elementary grades.[6] Like the early Pressey teaching machines, systems of drill, or drill and practice, are auxiliary to the general, nonmechanized instructional process. The computer, through printout, visual display, or audio message, presents the student with problems and questions based on the material that the teacher has presented in class. The student types in the answer at his or her console, or indicates it with a light pen and cathode ray tube. The computer evaluates the answer and informs the student whether his or her answer is correct. The main difference from the teaching machine is the computer's capacity to incorporate a number of study tracks of varying difficulty and to move the student along these tracks as his or her performance dictates. The utility of drill and practice systems has been most evident in areas such as spelling and elementary math, which call for laborious drills that are not only distasteful to the teacher but irksome to students performing either more rapidly or more slowly than the pace that is presupposed by one-track drills.

Tutorial systems differ from drill and practice systems in their comprehensiveness. At best, they structure an integrated instructional enterprise so that, for example, a student could develop proficiency in reading through exposure to the system only. In the tutorial system the teacher, not the computer, plays an auxiliary role, guiding students who have encountered difficulty with the program. Tutorial systems are necessarily driven by more sophisticated programs. The computer is not confined to evaluating a response as correct or incorrect and can accommodate "constructed responses" that may range over a broad set of possibilities. It can inform the student not only that his or her answer is wrong, but *why* it is wrong. Present tutorial systems are, however, hampered by many technical difficulties in program design.

Technical difficulties of a still higher order surround the development of computer programs for dialogue systems in which student and computer engage in a subject-specific but otherwise open-ended dialogue. The difficulty inheres not only in programming the computer to anticipate a virtually limitless range of questions. Problems lie, too, in enabling the computer to comprehend the natural language in which the questions are typed at the console and, particularly for the lower elementary grades, enabling the computer to understand the sentences spoken by students not yet trained to write.

Not all uses of the computer in education need to be so grand in scale. Researcher Seymour Papert believes that it is important to teach children how "to think, to learn, to plan," and that these objectives can be accomplished through computational mathematics, such as a form of mathematics that he calls "turtle geometry." At the heart of turtle geometry is a computer language, LOGO, developed by Papert and his associates, that children use to program the movements of a "turtle"—"a cybernetic toy capable of moving forward or back in a particular direction and of rotating about a central axis." In the process of programming the turtle, the children learn turtle geometry, a mathematics that, "although completely formal and rigorous ... is very close to the intuitive geometry one can assume a child will have acquired informally." According to Papert, turtle geometry teaches heuristic skills, involves students in controlling physical processes, is based on an intuitive, discovery approach to problem solving, and teaches students how to apply mathematical models to real life situations.[7] The software advances of turtle geometry, like so many of the hardware advances already described, came from outside the instructional materials industry—in this case from research pursuits in artificial intelligence.

These systems of computer-assisted instruction are still largely in the experimental stage. The popular view that the computer has already made significant inroads on the schooling process probably stems from its other applications, such as its computational use by students and its use for retrieval of data or for simulation and gaming exercises. While such uses have achieved more than experimental success, they are characteristically found in higher rather than elementary education.

Like teaching machines, systems of computer-assisted instruction have enjoyed only a limited acceptance in the public schools. A 1970 study reports that less than 1,000 terminals for computer-assisted instruction serve less than 20,000 public school students.[8] The reasons for restraint differ, however, from those applicable to teaching machines. One reason is that programming for computer-assisted instruction is still largely in the experimental stage. Another is that the unit costs of computers and consoles are high, more on the order of investment in buildings than in audiovisual equipment. School systems are naturally disinclined to make such a large capital expenditure with so tenuous a software base. Also, because the systems are still largely experimental, estimates of their productivity can only be speculative.

Estimates of hardware and software costs vary widely, over a range of at least one order of magnitude.[9] But even at the lower end of this range of estimates, costs will be high enough to require some reassessment of the proportion of the public school budget allotted to instructional materials. At the same time, the costs of implementation may, for several reasons, be lower than the common range of estimates. Software costs are usually figured per school or per district. In fact they should be distributed over all schools that have the hardware to use them. A math drill and practice program can be used with equal facility at any number of sites. The hardware figures appear to assume the need for mainframe computers on site, and to have ignored the economies to be derived from time sharing and more advanced computer communications systems that, by reducing present communications costs, will make it feasible for a district to rely on a distant computer to bring total cost well below that of an on-site computer.

Also, sources of support for research in improving the efficiency of computer-assisted instruction are not confined to the education sector. Research in diverse fields of artificial intelligence will probably continue to produce findings that can be put to instructional uses. Finally, experiments with applied computer-assisted instruction can be expected to produce results relevant to the instructional process generally and may be used to improve traditional texts and instructional techniques. Generalized, these findings may provide the opportunity for truly innovative and efficient uses of the computer in instruction, and its liberation from the simulation of traditional teaching techniques to which it is now confined.

Software: Instructional Content

Instructional hardware reflects innovation in fields ranging from printing technology and film production to computer manufacture. Although many teachers and schools have resisted the introduction of some of these devices, particularly those that require training and planning, there is a market for advances in hardware design. But what of advances in instructional materials' *content*? Like Papert's turtle, programs of computer-assisted instruction are only in their infancy, and much stands between the present state of the art and the effective introduction of these approaches into the nation's schools.

Advances in instructional technique have gained their widest acceptance in principle, not in practice. Parents, schools and teachers readily agree on instructional approaches to be taken in the classroom but resist the adoption of materials that concretely incorporate these techniques. The inquiry approach is a good example. This approach, widely believed to hold prospects for increasing the quality of education, transcends the division between those who believe that education should communicate content and those who believe that it should communicate process, teaching students how, as well as what, to think. Yet, programs premised on the inquiry approach have generally failed.

Inquiry as an instructional method has its modern origins in the work of John Dewey. Dewey believed that "thinking is the method of an educative experience." Among the method's essentials were that "the pupil have a genuine situation of experience—that there be a continuous activity in which he is interested for its own sake"; that "a genuine problem develop within this situation as a stimulus to thought"; and that "suggested solutions occur to him which he shall be responsible for developing in an orderly way."[10] Although some have found in Dewey a devotion to method that sacrifices content, Dewey in fact "always insisted that method could not be divorced from content. The subject matter and the means of communicating it were inexplicably bound together; and a successful performance depended upon a mastery of both."[11]

The wide favor won by Dewey's ideas is suggested by their currency in the rhetoric and practices of the major midcentury educational reform movements. Efforts to attain educational excellence in the late 1950s claimed content and process as their distinctive concerns. Attempts to communicate the structure of knowledge characterized this movement's concern for instructional content, while attempts at encouraging students to an inductive or discovery approach characterized its instructional process. A second movement, which originated in the mid-1960s, struck a distinctly humanistic theme and, responding to perceived problems of race, poverty, and student alienation, produced "free" and "open" schools whose curricula, though they heavily emphasized intellectual discovery and personal interaction, also made a place for drills and memorization in the instruction of basic reading and math. The "back-to-basics" movement, which apparently developed in reaction to the first two, stressed the school's role in conveying basic subject matter to students but also, at least in its rhetoric, left ample room for the school to teach students how to think.

Agreement on principle did not, however, mean agreement on technique. Programs incorporating the inquiry method encountered many obstacles in the school market; the few to survive were those that least threatened the status quo.

As related by one reviewer, Odvard Dyrli, the inquiry-oriented laboratory programs which were introduced in the 1960s, such as *Science—A Process Approach*, contrasted sharply with the then existing textbooks, most of which "tended to emphasize acquisition of the most arbitrary trivia—the memorization of terms, facts, definitions—and the quick recall of stored bits of knowledge." Their publishers responded with largely cosmetic, revised editions in which, among "the usual italicized terms, we now found a sprinkling of process words: *inferring, predicting*, making hypotheses." At about this time, however, many schools were already beginning to abandon the more costly elements of the laboratory programs. Shrinking budgets and the dawning recognition that "children and lab programs were now doers but *not* readers," produced demands for a new generation of textbooks that would economize on science programs and communicate content as well as promote inquiry. At least by Dyrli's measures, the efforts of this second generation are only slightly less ineffectual than those of the first. A small handful showed marked progress.[12]

Resistance to instructional materials that implemented the inquiry approach came from a number of sources. The widely held belief that social studies courses should instill patriotism was apparently one barrier to the adoption of programs that, through inquiry, appeared to encourage skepticism about traditional faiths.[13] The experience of one science program, Science Research Associates' *Inquiry Development Program in Physical Science (IDP)*, suggests that resistance to the inquiry approach stemmed from its practicalities rather than its principle. Teachers appear to have resisted the program because they were ill prepared to execute it and because they were anxious about its implications for their control of the classroom.[14]

IDP was based on research conducted by Dr. J. Richard Suchman at the University of Illinois. As developed by Science Research Associates, working with Dr. Suchman, the program was designed for grades 6 through 9 as a basic one-year course in physical science or as a supplement to science programs already in the curriculum. The program's elements included twenty-five 8mm silent film loops, a teacher's guide, and testing materials. The program was first marketed in 1966 and last actively promoted in 1972.

Under the program's format, a film loop, a teacher demonstration, or a picture in the student's *Idea Book* would present a puzzling physical event—such as a metal blade which, when heated, bent upwards. Teacher and student would then inquire into the reasons for the event. As originally planned by Suchman, students were only to ask questions answerable by "Yes" or "No." This regimen was soon modified to allow teachers to give more directed answers, but teachers were still enjoined not to lecture in the traditional fashion. Students were also encouraged to look for answers by using their experimental kits and the resource book.

IDP required teachers to shift their role from expositor, delivering knowledge, to advisor, assisting in the search for knowledge. Obviously this demanded a substantial personal investment. Learning a new type of instruction was only the first hurdle. Teachers also had to face the prospect of diminished classroom control, because students would simultaneously be pursuing disparate, often noisy activities, and because they would be free to ask questions for which the teacher would have no ready answer. Also, for those teachers without a solid grounding in physical science, the publisher suggested review of a basic physics text. The elementary grade teacher, not characteristically a subject matter specialist, would have to spend time acquiring the needed substantive knowledge.

Both *IDP* and *Science—A Process Approach* were structured around the inquiry approach. Why did one fail where the other succeeded? One difference is that *S-APA* left the teacher at the center of the classroom, while *IDP*, with its individualized and open-ended processes, threatened teacher control. Teachers received considerably more training and preparation for use of *S-APA*; they also needed it less for *S-APA* than for *IDP*.

The testing mechanisms that accompanied *S-APA* gave teachers the security of knowing how their students were performing. *IDP*'s initial position was that traditional testing contradicts the purposes of the inquiry approach. (Subsequently, in an effort to alleviate teacher anxiety, *IDP*'s publisher abandoned this position and provided a Student Response Booklet containing true-false questions, and a teacher handbook explaining how to interpret student responses and classroom behavior generally.) In short, the difference between the two programs is that where *IDP* sought to stimulate inquiry as an open-ended process, *S-APA* sought only to simulate it with an intensely structured, routinized program.

Measuring Materials' Performance

AAAS conducted carefully structured pilot tests of *S-APA*, giving schools some indication of the results that might be expected among different populations. These efforts set *S-APA* apart not only from *IDP*, but from instructional materials generally. Although many obstacles stand in the way of innovation, a fundamental problem is the lack of information about how, and how well, instructional products perform. Facing the risk of failure, and having no indication of the extent of the risk, schools are naturally disinclined to acquire materials that take off in new directions.

Few techniques have been developed for measuring the efficacy of instructional materials, much less their capacity for increasing student productivity. It is much easier to measure the performance of hardware than software. And producers have little incentive to invest in testing their materials, because the school systems with which they deal have no stake in improving student performance or requiring proof that materials will contribute to such improvement. Nor, for the same reason, do producers have incentive to invest in overcoming the methodological hurdles that surround the testing effort.

Methodological Hurdles

Attempts at systematically evaluating the efficacy of instructional materials date back at least fifty years. They surfaced in the early 1960s as part of the renewed interest in programmed materials. Captivated by the technological possibilities, instructional program producers viewed evaluation as a necessary element of quality control and as a vehicle for attaining larger insights: "finding out what students actually learn and remember from the program."[15] The motives underlying this concern are understandable. Because these programs were to be largely self-administered by students, with little if any teacher interaction, the usual controls represented by ongoing teacher assessment of materials' efficacy would be missing. At the same time, the context of such measurement was methodologically appealing, for the absence of teachers implied the exclusion of a significant variable in the measurement of instructional materials' efficacy.

Other serious methodological obstacles continue to stand in the way of effective materials testing. Attempts to measure the efficacy of materials in a single classroom setting, without isolating external influences, are unsatisfactory for their limited predictive values. Yet true laboratory conditions, with significant external influences controlled, are practically unattainable. Classroom and teacher influences can be excluded, but a number of possibly more important factors, such as background, experience, and ability of the individual subjects, will be elusive and indeterminate. And even if they could be obtained, these naked assessments of materials' efficacy would be of little use to school systems, which must decide whether the materials would be effective in classrooms crowded with the very factors excluded by the experiment.

The instruments being used to evaluate materials range widely in their sensitivity to methodological difficulties. One instrument apparently assumes that efficacy for students can be measured exclusively by the reactions of the teacher and other nonstudent experts. Another instrument recognizes that in fact there may be a negative correlation between expert speculation and student measures, and proposes a systematic method for directly evaluating effect on students.[16] Yet another approach calls for a staged process, beginning with premarket verification of a product's efficacy, at which point the producer "has learned some but not all of the important things about what his product will do with certain students," to a postadoption period, as the product enters a variety of classroom environments. Methodological uncertainties would be resolved progressively as inquiry focused on such questions as:

What internal elements of the materials present difficulties to what sorts of learners?

What unanticipated situational problems are being encountered by what sorts of school users, and how can the materials be adapted or supplemented to solve these problems?

How many of the product's shortcomings in specific situations are due not to faults in its internal elements or design, or to things that may be corrected through adaptation, but to lack of specific training for the teachers?[17]

These approaches should begin to suggest the nature of the methodological obstacles to measuring materials' efficacy. Even without these obstacles, the institutional barriers to effective measurement seem insurmountable under present conditions.

Legislative Efforts

Efforts to legislate these institutional barriers away seem destined to fail. California and Florida were the first states to seek to compel publishers to verify the efficacy of their materials. California's 1972 legislation requires that publishers and manufacturers "develop plans to improve the quality and reliability of instructional materials through learner verification." They "shall provide copies of test results and evaluations made as part of learner verification at the request of any governing board," and governing boards "shall be encouraged to permit publishers and manufacturers to have limited access to classrooms for necessary testing and observation."[18]

"Learner verification" is defined by the California statute as "the continuous and thorough evaluation of instructional materials for their effectiveness with pupils."[19] One advocate of learner verification, testifying before California's Curriculum Development and Supplemental Materials Commission, characterized learner verification as "the empirical process of data gathering and analysis by which the instructional effectiveness of the curriculum materials may be determined before they reach the market and then continuously monitored, examined, and improved upon during their life cycle."[20]

The California statute is less than crystalline on a number of points. Far from requiring or even addressing verification procedures categorically, it only requires publishers to "develop plans." The extent and nature of the mandated plans are left unclear, and the sanctions for noncompliance are not specified. Presumably if a publisher does not comply with the statute, state and district boards are to refuse to consider or purchase its materials. There is support for this position in the statute and in administrative procedures adopted subsequent to its enactment.[21] The Board of Education's May 1975 *Call For Bids* required among other things that publishers "submit information on learner verification already performed or their plans to conduct such verification."

While the statute itself offers no principled basis for the development of in-school verification techniques, draft guidelines have been developed by a Learner Verification Committee consisting of officials of California's Department of Education, the Curriculum Development and Supplemental Materials Commission, local school administrators and representatives of educational publishers. The guidelines define learner verification to mean "simply that the publisher determines and reports the answers to two questions: 1. For what purpose was the material designed? 2. How well was the purpose achieved when the pupils used it?"

The guidelines propose that the publisher, together with the school where the materials will be tested, assess in advance their shared requirements, limitations and procedures. This assessment should cover, among other topics, the needs of pupils, the purpose of the materials (such as skill and concept development), performance objectives, and necessary testing activities. The publisher and school district should also conduct necessary in-service training for the teachers involved. The guidelines list twenty questions for evaluating the evaluation. Among them are: What instrument, control group and sampling will be used? How well was the material taught? What "criterion measures" were used to judge the product's effectiveness? Who conducted the test? What socioeconomic levels, ethnic groups and age groups were tested?

Under the guidelines, the publishers are to provide "free copies of necessary instructional materials and tests and other evaluation instruments." The guidelines give the publisher considerable freedom to select the appropriate vehicle for evaluation but do specify one classroom of thirty students as a minimum number of respondents in any verification. In reporting the findings of a learner verification, the publisher "is expected to state the learning objectives, type of pupil for which the particular material is best suited, and the percentages of pupils who can profit from the use of such materials."[22]

The Florida learner verification statute, enacted in 1974, offers a contrast to the California provisions. In addition to attempting a more detailed definition of learner verification, the Florida legislation requires a showing that materials have been revised in light of learner verification results and includes within its concept of revision "specific revision of the materials themselves, revision of the teacher's materials, and revision of the teacher's skills through retraining."[23]

Unlike California's statute, which requires only the development of plans for learner verification, the Florida law requires that publishers submit "written proof of the use of the learner verification and revision process during prepublication development and postpublication revision of the materials in question." If the publisher is unable to provide this proof, and "wishes to submit material for adoption, he must satisfy the state instructional materials selection council that he will systematically gather and utilize learner verification data to revise the materials in question to better meet the needs of learners throughout the state."

As suggested by their imprecise drafting, learner verification statutes have been hastily considered and have ignored hard questions. If schools genuinely wanted effective materials, they would have required verification on their own, without statutory prompting, as a condition to purchasing materials from a producer. Can legislation make purchasers less indifferent? If it can, and if verification programs prove effective, is there any reason to believe that verification results will identify student needs any more accurately than unaided purchaser decisions?

There are other problems. Widespread emphasis on learner verification instruments and student attainment of specified objectives may well encourage producers to direct their investment toward development of materials that test well but do not necessarily teach well. Also, little attention has been paid to the question whether the benefits of learner verification are worth its added costs.

Alternatives to statutorily mandated learner verification do exist. A not-for-profit clearing house, the Educational Products Information Exchange Institute, has been formed to provide independent product evaluations to its client schools. Among its other activities, EPIE has worked with a lay group to develop product review criteria for parents and concerned citizens generally.[24] EPIE's apparent aim is to serve, for schools and instructional materials, the kind of function served by Consumers Union for consumers and consumer goods generally.

Arguments for mandated learner verification met an early flurry of enthusiasm from legislators and resistance from some publishers. Over the long run, learner verification programs, whether mandated by statute or administered by private organizations like EPIE, can be expected to have only a modest effect on the level and direction of investment in instructional materials research and development. The obvious reason is that learner verification does not begin to touch the prevailing forces that shape purchaser preference and producer response and that steer investment away from large or differently focused instructional advances. Learner verification does nothing to ameliorate the problems of appropriability that discourage investment by producers and schools alike. Nor can it do anything to alter the generally conservative patterns of materials selection decisions.

3   How Instructional Materials Are Purchased

The consumers of instructional materials are overwhelmingly conservative in their preferences. Given a choice between materials closely patterned after the ones they now use and materials that mark a sharp departure in teaching technique, they will typically prefer the first. This conservatism pervaded even the late 1950s and early 1960s, when the innovative spirit was at its height in the nation's schools.

A massive inventory of innovations in New York's public schools revealed that "despite their increased rate of instructional innovation, the great bulk of schools as structured institutions had remained stable." According to the inventory, most changes "involved an alteration in subject content (ordinarily different information and more of it), in instructional material (usually a new textbook), or in the grouping of pupils (most commonly class reduced or varied classes). Few programs embody changes in the kind of people employed, in the way they were organized to work with students, in the nature of instructional materials they used, or in the kinds of places in which they were taught."[1]

This resistance stems in part from the fact that school organizations have no reason to purchase innovative instructional products. Increases in educational efficiency are not needed to attract students and fill classrooms. The compulsory attendance laws provide a captive market, and private schools offer little competition. Indeed, schools have every reason *not* to purchase innovative materials. Particularly in the elementary grades, schools are widely perceived as serving the crucial function of preparing students to become part of America's ongoing political and social life. This perception, with its emphasis on the status quo, is not likely to invite experimentation.

Schools are subject to many internal and external forces which influence their decisions in conservative directions. In selecting instructional materials, classroom teachers bend to the will of principals, superintendents, school boards, voters, state agencies and legislatures. These individuals and institutions in turn yield to the power of each other and of the teacher. Each relevant group has power approximating a substantive veto over decisions of the others. The diversity of individuals and groups whose interests must be satisfied in the selection of materials suggests that materials designed to avoid the objections of all will be bland. This blandness is reinforced by the requirement in many states that materials be uniform throughout the state.

The critical point is not that any single group seeks to have the final say in the process of selecting instructional materials, but that many seek to have some say. In a recent survey of seventy-two representatives from a wide variety of organizations concerned with public schooling, the transcendent desire was to be consulted and involved in the making of curricular decisions. Representatives from organizations as diverse as the National Congress of Parents and Teachers, the American Association of School Administrators, the American Council on Education, the National Council for Social Studies, the National Organization for Women, and the American Federation of Teachers submerged their concern for what should be taught, and how, to an overriding interest in having "a piece of the action at all levels of curriculum decision-making."[2]

The interests of these groups are far from homogenous. Instructional materials must fill criteria set by educational professionals and by outsiders. The public may be generally uninformed about the processes and substance of selection decisions, but this does not mean that it is disinterested or without influence. According to a Gallup poll on public attitudes toward education, "there is great interest in the very areas that most school publicity presently neglects—the content of courses and the educational process versus school operation."[3] The public's greatest influence lies in its silence, and in professional decisions to reject materials that will spark controversy and rouse the public from this silence.

Professionals also divide over the standards to be applied in materials selection. Some educators favor traditional teaching methods, while others prefer more innovative techniques. As Kirst and Walker have observed, "even those who agree that truths honored in our tradition should shape the curriculum may still disagree over whether certain classics should be taught in the English or Latin translation or in the original Greek. They may argue over whether to include Vergil together with Tacitus and Julius Caesar in a fixed course of study. They may differ over the amount of time to be allotted to the Bible and other more strictly oriented texts."[4]

Innovation is also dulled by a large and growing number of external forces. Testing and accreditation, to take just two examples, exert a uniformly leveling influence. A school that wants to maintain its performance level on any of the national standardized reading and math examinations will not be inclined to experiment with new instructional techniques in those areas. Because they are the first rungs on the public school ladder, the elementary grades are also indirectly subjected to influences operating on the higher grades. Elementary schools must provide the foundations for the skills tested by statewide achievement exams and by the College Board examinations. Schools must also meet the standards established by regional accrediting organizations, standards that characteristically attach little value to instructional innovation.[5]

The forces affecting instructional materials selection are many and varied. State statutes prescribing selection standards and methods only begin to indicate the forces at work. The structure of materials selection is open textured, enabling voters, special interest groups, boards of education, school administrators, and teachers to have a part in these decisions. Because of this interplay, the materials selected will satisfy the lowest common denominator among the interests expressed.

Organizations and Change

The preamble to one materials selection law declares that "because of the common needs and interest of the citizens of this state and the nation, there is a need to establish broad minimum standards and general educational guidelines for the selection of instructional materials for the public schools." At the same time, the preamble recognizes "that, because of economic, geographic, physical, political, educational, and social diversity, specific choices need to be made at the local level."[6]

The formal balance between state and local control has been struck differently across the country. In the so-called adoption states, major responsibility for selecting materials is lodged in state agencies. In the nonadoption states, the main authority is vested in largely autonomous school districts or other local government units. By recent count, there are twenty-one adoption states, situated predominantly in the south, southwest and far west, and twenty-nine nonadoption states, mostly situated in the northeast, midwest and northwest.[7]

It is easy to attach too much weight to the adoption and nonadoption categories. Selection decisions are exclusively centralized or decentralized in only a very few states. Thus in some adoption states, the responsible state agency selects texts and other materials, leaving little or no discretion to local districts; in others, the state agency approves a long list of texts, giving local districts discretion to choose from the list and to purchase supplementary materials chosen entirely on their own but with reimbursement from the state. Parallel differences also exist among nonadoption states.

Compromises between state and local control are also achieved outside the materials selection laws. Even if a local board has complete autonomy in buying its materials, it may be constrained by curriculum decisions reached at the state level. In many states, statutes prescribe the course of study to be followed throughout the state, and sometimes specify the grades in which courses are to be taught and the sequence to be followed. More eclectic statutory provisions are also influential. Some require instruction in patriotism, in kindness to animals, or in contributions made by minority groups. Others prohibit denominational references or require treatment of the Confederacy. Statutory requirements frequently call for the presentation of materials on the history of the state and sometimes on regional and local history.

In New York, a nonadoption state, the Education Department's Bureau of Elementary Curriculum Development distributes a handbook, *An Overview of Suggested Procedures for Improving Methods of Textbook Selection*, which outlines criteria for text selection and procedures for the formation of local text selection committees. The bureau also distributes Curriculum Guides for science, math, English, language arts and social studies. These guides, produced by committees of teachers and subject area specialists under the supervision of administrators from the bureau, provide "recommended" or "suggested" course outlines. Each guide includes a short list of books for teacher reference. Some expressly identify pertinent instructional materials.

Local Organization for Materials Purchase

In all but the most centralized adoption states, local boards will select materials from a list approved by the state, or even on their own. Though the decisions are made locally, they are by no means insulated from the influence of many individuals and groups. In California, for example, district boards are required to "provide for substantial teacher involvement and shall promote the involvement of parents and other members of the community in selecting instructional materials."[8]

Local school organizations consist of three groups, each possessing some responsibility for instructional materials selection—teachers, school administrators, and the board of education. At the periphery are the voters, to whom the organization is responsible. Teachers probably play the central role in local decisions on what instructional materials get used in class, through their participation on selection committees and through their control of classroom activities. Administrators affect instructional materials selection mainly through their efforts at initiating curricular and organizational change. Boards of education typically spend little time on curriculum and still less on instructional materials. Voters spend even less time, if any at all, on these two questions. Yet if for some reason the board or the public strongly object to the instructional materials being used in their schools, each has the power to exercise a veto and have the materials removed.[9]

Within any local school organization, these three groups will splinter into many more, increasing the difficulty of reaching the consensus needed to introduce materials that will significantly alter instruction. Consider, for example, the channels for local decision described in the manual *Selecting Instructional Materials for Purchase*, issued by the Joint Committee of the National Education Association and the Association of American Publishers. According to the manual, a selection committee consisting predominantly of teachers will issue recommendations "by vote or by consensus of the members. Dissenting points of view, if any, should be treated with respect, aired and passed on for consideration by faculty and administrators." These recommendations are then to be cleared with a variety of officials, including principals, department chairpersons, subject matter supervisors, the curriculum or instructional council, the local educational association and its officers, the assistant or associate superintendent in charge of instruction, and the business officer and others concerned with budget. Before presenting the recommendation to the board of education, the superintendent may seek additional information and assurances that "the selection will have the approval of, or will not be subjected to criticism or attack by, representatives of the public."[10]

A look at the practices of three New York school districts will add some detail.[11] The timetable for selection in the city district observed begins anywhere between September and April, when subject area supervisors and curriculum evaluation committees formally identify subject areas in which new materials are needed. Textbook selection committees are then formed. The district's *Procedure for Selecting Textbooks* provides that these committees be "composed of principals, teachers, and supervisors from the areas concerned— elementary, academic, and vocational." "Application for Participation" forms are posted in teachers' rooms throughout the district and solicit information about employment status (contract, probationary, or temporary), number of years of teaching experience, and availability for committee meetings in the city during summer recess.

Early in May an announcement is sent "to all known publishers of textbooks, school reference books, and instructional materials, indicating the areas to be reviewed, and the name of the chairperson of each committee," and requesting the submission of all possibly relevant materials to the respective committee chairpersons. Between July and August, the textbook committees meet to evaluate the materials submitted, and committee members hear presentations by salespersons and consultants from the publishing companies.

A parallel, informal activity which has developed in the district seems to exert an important gateway influence on the range of materials eventually reviewed by the selection committees. It is apparently district policy to discourage salespersons from contacting individual teachers. Instead they are directed to one official in the district's Division of Curriculum Evaluation and Development. Throughout the year, this official received publishers' brochures and new instructional materials and distributes them to supervisors, and sometimes to teachers, who in the official's judgment are best situated to evaluate them. This official also keeps a file of publishers for use by text selection committees, administers the selection of these committees, and compiles annual editions of the approved textbook lists. It is her job to appear before the school board to defend the composite recommendation of the text selection committees, the associate superintendent for instructional services, and the superintendent of schools.

In the suburban New York district observed, the supervisor of the district's curriculum development office played a similarly central role in forming committees and coordinating text selection. In this district, the first step was for the supervisor to notify all teachers that a committee was being formed and to solicit their interest. After consulting with principals, the supervisor selected a committee that was in his opinion balanced in terms of age, experience, and educational philosophy. The supervisor provided each committee with a "charge to the committee," outlining the main issues and areas to be considered. Later, committee members analyzed curricular and text goals and undertook in-service training from consultants, from a local university, or from other school districts. When its training was completed, the committee formulated an evaluation instrument against which to measure the texts submitted.

Shortly after forming the committees, the supervisor ordered examination copies, so that by the time the in-service training was completed a minimum of fourteen or fifteen sets of materials would be available for examination by committee members. Members then individually completed evaluation instruments for each book or materials set. The data contained in the completed instruments were tabulated in the curriculum office and the results reviewed by the supervisor, who eliminated any materials receiving uniformly low ratings. At this point the committee met to review the completed evaluation instruments and sift the results until seven or eight books or sets of materials remained. A consultant from each of the respective seven or eight publishing companies was then invited to make a presentation to the committee.

The selection of materials in the rural New York district studied differs from selection practices in the city and suburban districts in a number of ways. Although classroom teachers were generally ineligible for appointment to text selection committees, they were encouraged to participate in committee deliberations, to an extent not observed in other districts. And although the district had not developed its own formal selection criteria, relying instead upon the state criteria, all texts that were considered seriously were subjected to "pilot projects" to determine their utility, a procedure not systematically followed in the other districts.

Although decision making in the rural district appeared to be less centralized, with principals assuming functions discharged by district-wide personnel in the city and the suburb, other factors led to district-wide uniformity. Selection committees consisted of subject area chairpersons from each of the district's five elementary schools. Appointed by the principals of their schools, these chairpersons were to represent their school's teachers on district-wide committees for curriculum revision and text selection in their subject areas. The text selection committees did not meet according to any specified timetable, but only when a need for revision was perceived by teachers, department chairpersons or principals. Once convened, the selection committees were charged with evaluating a broad range of materials, consulting in the process with teaching, administrative, and library staff, and with representatives from publishers whose texts were being considered.

State Organization for Materials Purchase

In 1972 California replaced its strict adoption system with a multiple adoption system, under which local school districts would select their materials from among several approved by the state Board of Education on recommendations made by the state's Curriculum Development and Supplemental Materials Commission.

The Curriculum Development and Supplemental Materials Commission stands at the head of a complex but informal statewide organization for evaluating instructional materials. In this role, "the Commission spends much of its time mediating pressures and claims from publishers, interest groups and their own evaluators," according to 1974 testimony before California's Senate Education Committee by Armin Rosencranz, a staff lawyer and social scientist at the Childhood and Government Project, University of California, Berkeley. Rosencranz's testimony continued, "Basically, the Commissioners react to the publishers' submissions, taking into account the claims of the interest groups, when possible. They hardly ever ask the larger questions, such as what ought the state to be doing in curriculum development and materials selections, and what ought to be included in curricula and materials."[12]

A brief itinerary of the materials selection process in California will suggest the variety of checks and balances at work in a system for choosing among products that, according to Rosencranz, "tend to be very similar, and similarly bland."

The biennial adoption cycle is initiated, usually in July, by the Education Department's publication of a call for bids and for submission of materials in a particular subject area. The call will state the governing legal and qualitative criteria developed by the commission and its advisory committees and approved by the Board of Education. Within two weeks of the call, producers must notify the Education Department of their intent to submit. Samples must be delivered to the department by the beginning of September, and price bids by the end of December. Although producers may have access to draft criteria before their formal adoption, this close timing indicates that the commission and its advisory committees generally frame their criteria to reflect the nature of materials already being used in California and elsewhere.

In the first stage of the selection process, a Legal and Factual Committee appointed by the commission reviews the submitted materials for compliance with the legal criteria (such as balanced portrayal of minority contributions) and for their factual accuracy. For these purposes, commissioners may also appoint their own Legal and Factual Analysis Committees from among teachers, school officials, and minority group representatives residing within the geographical area that the commissioner represents.

At the next stage, scheduled to take four to five months, materials are screened for instructional quality. Committees formed by individual commissioners conduct the review at this stage and are often aided by subcommittees and even sub-subcommittees. Each sub-subcommittee or subcommittee is expected to report back to its governing committee, which in turn provides its commissioner with reports and tabulated short answer forms for presentation to the entire commission. Hundreds, even thousands, of local teachers, school officials, and special interest group representatives become involved in the work of these evaluation teams, some on their own initiative and others by invitation.

Samples of submitted materials are circulated among the evaluation teams, with round-robin procedures devised for the dissemination of more bulky or costly nontext materials. In some cases, publishers will be invited to demonstrate the use of their materials, while in others the commissioner or the evaluating team may insist that publishers have no contact with the evaluators. Evaluators may ask publishers to provide the results of preuse pilot tests conducted by the publishers; publishers may in turn seek permission from local districts to test their materials in selected district classrooms.

The commission reviews these reports and within a month selects a final list of instructional materials to present to the Board of Education for adoption. The board then completes its review over a three-month period. At its first monthly meeting during this period it receives the recommendations of the commission and approves the commencement of a thirty-day public display period mandated by statute as a prerequisite to final adoption.[13] At its next monthly meeting the board holds a public hearing, at which anyone may speak on the materials proposed for adoption. At its third monthly meeting, the board is expected to vote on the commission's recommendations for the adoption.

From the announcement of the call for bids to the board's final action, roughly one year will have elapsed. Yet the process of actually placing approved materials in the classroom has, in fact, only begun. When it renders its final adoption decision, the board will authorize the state Department of Education to negotiate contracts with the publishers whose materials have been adopted and to solicit orders from local school districts.

Converging Forces: The Creationist Controversy in California

In 1969 California's smoothly rolling text selection process was disrupted by a prolonged controversy over proposed criteria requiring that science texts present the creationist view of human origins alongside the existing, if implicit, evolutionist view. The controversy galvanized many forces that may also be concerned with questions of instructional technique. It is no surprise that at least one text proffered by the creationist advocates portrayed biology as an established body of knowledge rather than as an object of process and student inquiry, instructional techniques encouraged since the 1960s by science education reformers.[14] The controversy was eventually resolved through a series of compromises among a wide variety of interested constituencies and organizations.

Instructional efficiency, unlike many other educational topics, such as the respective places to be occupied by the evolutionist and creationist views of human origins, is not the sort of object that attracts active advocacy or sharply defined constituencies. Aside from the few empirical studies already noted, and some others to be discussed in connection with teacher behavior, there is little direct evidence on the ways in which school organizations reach decisions about the innovation to be sought in instructional materials. The creationist-evolutionist controversy offers an instructive analogy in revealing the play of contending forces on issues considered important to the schooling process.

The first seeds of the controversy were planted in Southern California early in the 1960s, when two Orange County housewives complained to their county school board that textbooks used in their children's schools wrongly portrayed evolution as a fact, rather than as a theory alongside which creationism had at least equal standing. Told that the schools could teach only what was in the textbooks, the two women in 1963 turned to California's Board of Education, which has ultimate responsibility for textbooks used in the state. They were joined in their effort by Walter E. Lammerts, the principal founder of the Creation Research Society. Together they succeeded in persuading the board to incorporate the following statement in its textbook policy:

Future state textbooks dealing with the subject of man's origins should refer to Darwinian evolution as an important scientific theory or hypothesis. California teachers should be encouraged to teach Darwinian evolution as theory rather than as a permanent, unchanging truth. . . .

The Board's action was unanimous.[15]

The policy statement apparently had little impact on the state's sixteen-member advisory committee on science education. In October 1969, the committee submitted a 205-page framework for science education in grades K–12. At least two members of the board objected to the framework's failure to incorporate the creationist approach. Their reasoning was that because the biblical story of creation "has never been proved wrong . . . we would be remiss if we didn't include it."[16] Board action on the framework was held over to the next month.

In the interim, public sentiment was aroused. Among the statements submitted to the board was one from Vernon L. Grose, a private citizen whose interest in the issue had been provoked by a newspaper item. At its 14 November meeting, the board voted to replace the passages of the framework dealing with evolution with two paragraphs from Grose's statement:[17]

All scientific evidence to date concerning the origin of life implies at least a dualism or the necessity to use several theories to fully explain relationships between established data points. This dualism is not unique to this study but is also appropriate in other scientific disciplines, such as the physics of light.

While the Bible and other philosophic treatises also mention creation, science has independently postulated the various theories of creation. Therefore, creation in scientific terms is not a religious or philosophic belief. Also note that creation and evolutionary theories are not necessarily mutual exclusives. Some of the scientific data (e.g., the regular absence of transitional forms) may be best explained by a creation theory, while other data (e.g., transmutation of species) substantiate a process of evolution.

The advisory committee objected to the amendment and asked the board to reconsider the issue, but without success. If the revised framework had its intended effect, science texts used in California's grades K–12 would soon give equal time to creationist views.[18]

Through November 1972 the Curriculum Development and Supplemental Materials Commission sought to apply the framework's general guidelines to the concrete task of text selection. The creationist view continued to be pressed. Among the texts submitted to the commission were some from the Creation Research Center. Yet the texts finally recommended by the commission in November did not differ substantially from those already in use.[19] At the same time, the commission informed the board that it had at least been able to agree on three specific guidelines for science texts. Assertions about evolution should be altered to conditional statements. The "how," but not the "ultimate causes," of origins should be considered, and questions not resolved in science should be posed to students to stimulate inquiry into the processes of science.[20]

According to a contemporary report in the journal *Science* the "Commission proposed to make editorial revisions in textbooks in accordance with these guidelines, and expected only a few changes to be necessary." Vernon Grose, who in the meantime had been appointed to the commission and put in charge of negotiating these changes with the text publishers, told *Science* that "for example, a textbook should not say an animal was adapted to its environment, since that would imply evolution. Either the publisher would have to replace 'adapted' by a neutral word," Grose said, "or he must state that the animal was 'either adapted to or designed for' its environment."[21]

After a November hearing attended by almost fifty speakers and a standing-room-only audience estimated at 500, the board met in mid-December to act on the texts proposed by the Curriculum Commission.[22] After voting down a motion that creation theory be included in the elementary science texts, the board agreed on a resolution substantially incorporating the guidelines proposed by the commission in November and conditioning adoption on the textbooks' compliance with the guidelines.

The task of editing "scientific dogmatism" out of the 135 approved texts fell to a special committee and subcommittee consisting respectively of three textbook specialists from the state Department of Education and two board members and two university-based scientists.[23] The committee made a preliminary report to the board at its 11 January meeting. In most cases, the committee sought only to qualify otherwise flat assertions about evolution. The statement, "It is known that life begins in the seas," would, for example, have been changed to "Most scientists believe that life may have begun in the seas." In one case the committee drafted a lengthy qualifying introduction to a chapter on evolution. At the same meeting, the board rejected a member's proposal that science texts be rewritten to include a paragraph specifically mentioning divine creation as one explanation of human origins.

In principle, the issue was settled in March when the board approved the proposed editorial qualifications. The editorial changes were incorporated in the texts after extensive consultation with Education Department staff. But it was one thing to reach compromise at a political level, quite another to convince interested constituencies that the change went far enough. In June 1975, more than two years after the board's action, the board postponed approval of forty science texts because of complaints that they presented evolution as a fact.

Another, more dramatic decision reached at the board's January meeting apparently had no impact at all on the content of instructional materials. The board's decision that specific discussion of creation theories be included in social science textbooks[24] went unheeded, as publishers resisted undertaking the more substantial effort of incorporating new information into their materials. As a consequence, adoption of social science texts has repeatedly been postponed because creationists object that the texts overlook creation theory.[25]

What does California's experience with the creationist controversy reveal about the forces affecting instructional materials selection? The main lesson is that political compromise will reduce instructional materials' content to its lowest, least offensive level. Attempts to reconcile a complex variety of contending forces led to criteria under which either no definitive statements are made (the criteria for science texts) or under which two equally definitive statements are made (the criteria for social science texts). Possibly appropriate for reconciling competitive views on human origins, neither approach is geared to the sustained adoption of single, dramatic instructional techniques.

The reason that the compromise was so broad is that the converging forces were so varied. Lined up against the inclusion of creation theory in elementary science texts were church leaders, state and national organizations, and prominent scientists, including nineteen of California's Nobel laureates. Resolutions protesting the board's position were passed by the Commission on Science Education of the AAAS, the American Chemical Society, and the National Academy of Sciences. The University of California's Academic Council, representing the University's faculty, called the creationist approach "a gross misunderstanding of the nature of scientific inquiry." The creationist side was fractionated, with a fundamental split between the Creation Research Society, which took a hard line against any teaching of evolution, and the more moderate American Scientific Affiliation, which was closely aligned with the position eventually adopted by the board.[26]

These and other groups also sought redress outside the board and the commission. Lawsuits and threats of lawsuits predominated. The Palo Alto School Board reportedly announced that it would seek an injunction against implementation of the amended 1969 framework,[27] and the National Association of Biology Teachers organized a defense fund for teachers who refused to follow the new guidelines. Viewing the board's 1973 compromise as a rebuff, one creationist group, Creation Education Equality, sought state legislation requiring that creation theory and evolution be given equal time in instructional materials and curriculum. At least one conservative Republican state assemblyman said that if the proposed legislation failed to pass he might sponsor an initiative to guarantee equal time for creationism.[28]

The media also played a role. The controversy was widely covered, in local newspapers, national magazines, religious periodicals, and science journals. Editorials appeared in a number of California newspapers. Indeed, it was an editorial in the *Los Angeles Times* that ostensibly prompted Vernon Grose to propose his framework amendment. Grose later had occasion to claim that the *Los Angeles Times* was inaccurate in its coverage of the dispute.[29] At least one board member issued a press release aimed at clarifying his own position. "I am frankly amazed at the wide diversity of interpretations of my public statements that I read and hear." The release continued, "The press, religionists, biologists and many others have reached conclusions so widely varied that I will attempt a succinct statement which is hopefully free from ambiguity."[30]

Ambiguity, however, was inherent in the task the board had set for itself and for the Curriculum Development and Supplemental Materials Commission. In recommending books for adoption under the 1969 framework the commission left unclear whether it interpreted the framework to require—or allow—mention of creation theory. And even after the Board voted the adoption "subject to any editorial changes that may be needed prior to contracting for the instructional materials," its members disagreed over the sort of editorial changes to be required. The board's vice-president expressed certainty that the books would be altered to include discussion of creation theories. Another board member, however, thought that the authorized changes only extended to qualification of flat assertions of scientific truth. This ambiguity left text publishers in a quandary as to the amount and kind of editing that they could safely undertake in the future.[31]

Ambiguity, indecision, and an attempt to accommodate all sides were the salient features of the California board's effort to grapple with the creation-evolution controversy. They were the most important features, too, in terms of their effects on publishers and on the content of instructional materials. Faced with an unclear directive, and one that might be reversed at any moment, publishers were reluctant to invest in change. They eventually yielded to the minor editorial adjustments adopted by the board, but staunchly resisted the requirement that they discuss creation in their social science texts. The lesson from this experience can probably be generalized to cover text selection in other states and instructional efficacy as well as content. The lesson paints a bleak picture for private investment in technical innovation, where publishers are being asked to invest much more on the basis of criteria that are far less certain or clear.

Teachers and Change

Teachers influence the content of instructional materials through their participation on selection committees, their advice to state and local officials and their role as gatekeepers to the classroom. Teacher participation in the selection of instructional materials has become a common subject of collective bargaining and is often guaranteed in agreements between school boards and teachers.[32] Teacher indifference or anxiety about a new product will mean that the product lies untouched on the storeroom shelf—if the product is acquired at all. Over the long run, producers will not invest in materials which do not generate enthusiasm and reorders.

Research on teacher reactions to the newer forms of instructional materials reveals attitudes ranging from indifference to anxiety. One study measuring teacher attitudes toward three types of instructional materials found that teachers preferred the more traditional types to the most innovative. Traditional teaching aids, such as flashcards, workbooks, and exercise books, received the most favorable response. Auxiliary instructional programs—programmed instruction, programmed text, and tutor text—were next. Strictly mechanized instructional programs involving automated instruction, mechanized tutor, and teaching machines received the least favorable response. More refined subsequent investigations by the same researchers confirmed that the threat of automation figured importantly in teacher attitudes toward instructional materials.[33]

Several studies on the criteria used by teachers in selecting instructional materials showed that concern for instructional efficiency occupied a low place or was not considered at all.[34] Teachers were instead concerned about the adaptability of materials to their instructional styles and the materials' practicality and attractiveness. Teachers expressed a preference for products that are easy to use, that include a teacher's manual, and that require little preparation. Concerns for content related mostly to surface qualities, such as factual accuracy, durability, attractiveness, and good illustrations, but also to instructional qualities, such as the appropriate organization of tasks. There was also some interest in the effects of materials on users—their ability to hold student interest and the time they required for the student to master the stated objectives.

Many factors explain teacher resistance and indifference to innovation. Some teachers are simply predisposed against educational innovation. Others may be pushed in that direction by their own educational and training experiences. Lack of a sustained commitment to the profession may be another cause for indifference. For some teachers, the classroom is a stopping-off point between college and raising a family. For others it is a long-term but low-paying job that must be supplemented with other, part-time employment. In neither setting can the teacher be expected to invest in honing his or her professional skills or generally in developing the commitment to the profession that may be necessary for him or her to advocate or even accept change.

For teachers who might otherwise be disposed to innovate, it may be significant that, at least in the elementary grades, they spend most of their working time with children. Contact with other teachers and with administrators is limited, and this situation hardly aids them in obtaining information about new products or, for that matter, about the extent to which instructional problems in their classrooms are duplicated in those of their colleagues. Teachers are apparently not encouraged to find time to identify and evaluate available instructional materials. According to a survey conducted by the Educational Products Information Exchange, teachers "spend only from three to ten hours per year selecting instructional materials, and a still smaller amount of time analyzing the instructional strengths and weaknesses of the materials prior to selecting them or putting them in the classrooms."[35]

Some of these conditions, such as marital and career patterns, may change over time. Others, such as teacher training programs, may be systematically improved with the objective of increasing teacher receptivity to innovation. Other conditions will be far more difficult to change. The most durable of these are conditions affecting teacher control of the classroom. These conditions affect not only the teacher's anxiety about loss of prestige but also his more positive, altruistic beliefs about education's appropriate nature and objects.[36]

These two key attitudes, anxiety and altruism, reinforce each other. For example, it has been found that feelings of inadequacy in the face of complex technology do not by themselves explain teacher resistance to computer-assisted instruction. Teachers also feel that, by introducing an element of impersonality, computer-assisted instruction will inhibit the environment for learning.[37]

Other examples abound and suggest the difficulty of uprooting these entrenched attitudes. One study of attempts to introduce programmed instruction into classroom activities found that, over a two-year period, the programs were eventually extended beyond their intended duration, and other adjustments were made so that teachers could spend more time with their students. The result, modifying programmed instruction to conform more closely to the characteristics of traditional instruction, was justified by teachers on the ground that "the students wanted more interaction with the teachers."[38] Another study found that teachers were preoccupied with maintaining control over student behavior and would resist inventions they thought might impair this control. Control was seen to be threatened not only by manifestly disruptive media or technologies but also by devices that might be used by students for their own purposes, unrelated to those that the teacher thought appropriate.[39]

The National Educational Association and the American Federation of Teachers appear to be less defensive about innovation than teachers generally. One survey of NEA and AFT leaders found that the NEA leaders canvassed were more favorable in their overall attitudes toward instructional media than was a reference group consisting of a representative sample of secondary and elementary school principals. The AFT leaders were somewhat less favorable in their attitudes than the administrators. The same study found that although instructional media "were not regarded by the majority of AFT and NEA leaders as 'threatening' to teachers," many leaders "were concerned about teacher voice in decision-making and the possible loss of classroom autonomy for the teacher if media were to be used extensively in the schools."[40]

Margins for Diversity

The intricate net of checks and balances involving students, teachers, administrators, and state and local agencies is one through which, it seems, little will pass that differs from what went before. Obviously the picture throughout the country, and even within states, districts, and schools, is not one of unrelieved uniformity. The present system may contain some areas in which change and diversity are possible.

Organizational innovativeness will vary among school systems and even among schools within a system. Receptivity to innovation has been shown to vary with such factors as a school district's spending, size, and complexity.[41] This means that if innovative schools or districts exist in sufficient number across the country, demand for innovative materials may exist at some level capable of repaying both the investment needed to produce them and the costs of identifying these receptive buyers.

Other possibilities for diversity exist. In the suburban New York district studied, the trend has been away from the adoption of a single basal text and toward multiple basal adoptions. The reason behind this shift was not to give the teacher a wider range from which to choose, but rather to enable the use of all books or series within the range in a single class, to accommodate the different abilities of students in the class. Thus, four or five basals have been selected in recent reading adoptions, one of which is strong on phonetics, another of which emphasizes comprehension. In social studies, selection committees often recommend six or seven basals for one grade level, in part because no single text covers all the desired subject matter, and in part because any single text assumes a range of class reading level that is narrower than the actual range in any class.

Teachers often assemble their own supplementary materials, ranging from mimeographed sheets to videotaped instructional units. Sometimes teachers are given allowances to supplement approved materials with products they choose themselves. The size of these allowances varies considerably, as do the procedures that a teacher must follow to obtain materials in this way. In the city district observed, the procedures were particularly burdensome and may explain the infrequency with which teachers took this path. A two-page purchase requisition had to be completed, reviewed by the district's financial office and by a supervisor in the subject area, and signed by the teacher making the requisition, the director of instruction, an associate superintendent, the director of the budget, and the purchasing agent.

Centralized libraries and instructional service institutions may also provide diverse and innovative materials at a price that school districts are willing to pay. In the city district studied, audiovisual materials are divided between a central film library and the individual schools. In addition to lending films, the library produces or purchases the film strips and transparencies that are stocked by the schools.

At least two or three of New York's fifty-four Boards of Cooperative Educational Services (BOCES) have attempted a considerably bolder entry into the development of curriculum and of instructional materials. BOCES occupy contiguous regions throughout the state. They are essentially service organizations, under annual contract to qualifying school districts within the region. The rural district studied had contracted for special educational and vocational services, for access to BOCES's extensive film and videotape libraries, and for home instruction and transportation for handicapped children.

The range of facilities provided by the one BOCES observed included an extensive film library (5,500 prints), videotape software and equipment, and an inventory of materials produced in the BOCES graphics department. These materials were like those sold commercially, and were provided by BOCES at less than half the commercial price. BOCES will also fill the requests of teachers in component school districts for custom-made charts and other graphics. BOCES's summer workshops may engage in custom crafting on a larger scale. Teachers have gathered in the BOCES shop to make up science kits patterned after commercial products. One kit, which contained little text and large amounts of manipulative materials, proved especially attractive. A group of teachers ordered one set of materials from the commercial producer and, after dissecting it, replicated the kit from odds and ends of equipment purchased from the five-and-dime store and from instructions that they paraphrased and reproduced by mimeograph. Although the economics of this kind of activity are attractive to schools and school districts, it will over the long run reduce publishers' incentives to invest in the development of these materials.

The Lowest Common Denominator?

A planner setting out to design a system guaranteed to discourage the purchase of innovative instructional materials would be hard pressed to improve on the system for materials selection that is followed throughout the country today. Although margins for efficacy and diversity do exist, the overwhelming preference is for the lowest, least unsettling common denominator in instructional materials content.

This pattern of preference stems from a concert of forces. Instructional materials selection is an open-textured process, inviting and accommodating the opinions and decisions of state lawmakers, state and local school administrators, teachers, parents and students, and the variety of organizations into which they group themselves. The fact that current patterns of consumer preference are formed from so many forces helps to explain their persistence and the futility of efforts to alter the pattern by altering one or even a handful of the elements that form it.

4

How Instructional Materials Are Produced

Orthodoxy in outlook and preference sets the tone for the instructional materials marketplace. Schools select materials conservatively because they have much to lose and little to gain by making innovative choices. In competing for school sales, publishers cannot be expected to introduce products that take off in new directions of instructional efficiency.

But consumer attitudes are only partly responsible for the prevailing direction and level of investment in invention. In an economic system that values private enterprise, industrial factors also have to be considered. It would be a mistake to ignore the many significant research and development implications of such factors as firm size, industry structure and the legal mechanisms available to producers for protecting their investments. Altering school structures to make them more receptive to change may be a necessary condition for significant investment in invention, but it is not a sufficient one.

The key disincentive to private investment in research and development is inappropriability. Because an invention is, once communicated, free for all to use, a firm cannot fully appropriate the invention's value to itself and will as a result have little reason to invest in research and development. A firm that produces a valuable invention can expect its competitors to incorporate the invention into their own products quickly and to price their products below the level needed to recoup the expenses of invention. As a consequence, the firm will probably not invest in invention in the first place.

The values of an invention are never completely inappropriable. Appropriability will vary with the nature of the invention, the size of the firm, and the structure of the industry within which the firm is situated. The legal mechanisms available to firms for capturing the value of their inventions will also naturally affect investment behavior. The mechanisms usually used for this purpose are the copyright, patent, and trade secret laws. Each in its own way enables the private appropriation of an invention's value by assuring the inventor a limited period during which he and he alone can practice his invention, to the exclusion of all competitors. The three laws differ in the kinds of subject matter they protect and in the level of protection they offer. As a consequence, their inducements to invention also differ.

Copyright law is commonly associated with the production and distribution of literature, musical composition, motion pictures and sound recordings. By its terms, the copyright law also embraces most forms of instructional materials—texts, workbooks, filmstrips, and audiovisual products. Yet the copyright law has been shaped with aesthetic rather than instructional productions in mind. Copyright protects expressions, but not their underlying ideas. It attracts investment to the expressive qualities that distinguish one work of art from another, but not to the kinds of ideas and techniques needed to make instructional materials more effective. In short, copyright protects most types of instructional materials, but its protection is not likely to induce investment in technical change.

Patent law, unlike copyright, is consciously aimed at protecting ideas and encouraging technical change. It is for quite different reasons that patent law will not attract investment to invention in instructional materials. The patent law has been interpreted to exclude protection for subject matter that depends for its operation on natural principles or human intervention, the hallmarks of instructional materials. Trade secret law, a close relative of patent law that is sometimes looked to for inducing investment in research and development, suffers its own peculiar shortcomings. It cannot of itself be expected to advance private investment in instructional materials research and development.

This chapter reviews the many industrial conditions affecting research and development investment by instructional materials producers. The clearest evidence of producer behavior is, of course, the direct evidence—how firms actually go about developing the products that they sell to schools. Yet firms are naturally reluctant to discuss practices that they believe are vital to their success, and the direct evidence is therefore sparse. The little direct evidence that is reliable is presented first. Less direct evidence—firm size, industry structure and the operation of the copyright, patent, and trade secret laws—follows.

Product Development

Textbooks

Typically, the development of a textbook begins with the identification by a firm's editors and outside consultants of a subject area and grade level in which a new textbook or series might be marketable. Discussion with sales personnel and inspection of competitors' products will play an important role at this stage.[1] Next, according to one publisher, come "several years of extensive research and writing, analysis of curricula, appropriate classroom testing, illustrations and production."[2] Design elements such as typography, illustrations, and preparations may claim as much as one-quarter of the textbook's cost. Design costs have recently increased dramatically, in part because of a penchant for color illustrations. The production of a text or text series may occupy anywhere from four to ten years.

The textbook publisher with a typical investment of $500,000 must sell 100,000 copies to break even.[3] These figures can be compared with those for an unillustrated, superficially edited trade book: typically, the trade book publisher can recover an investment of $35,000 with a sale of 11,000 copies. Furthermore, the investment by the publisher of textbooks for use in grades K–8 will often exceed $500,000. The step-by-step instructional progression characteristic of the curriculum in grades 1–6 requires the production of a series of six textbooks in each subject covered, together with allied workbooks and teacher guides. One basic reading series has eighty-nine elements—eleven basic readers, nineteen workbooks, and seven teachers' manuals among them.[4] The investment in a series of this scale can easily exceed $3 million. Throughout, the object is to reach and to satisfy the largest possible number of consumers. Large quantities of complimentary examination copies are distributed to teachers, and editing is aimed at meeting the interests of the widest audience.

The supervising editor oversees the textbook's development. He or she is responsible for soliciting text manuscripts or outlines from outside authors, who are often educators well known from their activities in professional associations. He or she then supervises the editorial staff's rewriting of manuscripts and outlines. Sometimes the editorial staff is assisted by subject matter and grade level specialists. Throughout the development process, the supervising editor's predominant concern will, in the words of one firm's manager, be "to achieve a compromise between the controls necessary for national acceptance and the originality of the author's contribution to education. In the elhi field particularly, he must balance skillfully the demands of contradictory curricular theory, of 'progressive educators' and traditional, or exponents of the science-centered culture and the humanists, and above all of the majority and minority pressure groups."[5]

It is hard to see how this balancing act can lead to other than modesty in the textbook's goals and objects. Instances can of course be cited in which text publishers have undertaken significant innovation in the design of instructional materials.[6] And, some publishers have asserted that they view it as part of their function to undertake or support basic research in learning theory, and to have their editorial staff kept "abreast of current research and attempt to incorporate its relevant findings into new materials."[7] But research and development that follows new avenues and aims at new objectives is only an occasional phenomenon in instructional materials research and development.

Audiovisual and Other Materials

The marriages between publishers and high-technology firms that took place in the 1960s were thought to augur a revolution in product development. General Electric and Time, Inc. heralded their formation of the General Learning Corporation with the announcement that "a major activity of the new enterprise would be research and development in the integrated use of editorial materials and new electronic technologies for both formal and informal education."[8] Bennet Cerf, chairman of Random House, commented on his company's acquisition by RCA, which had a special division devoted to the educational uses of electronics: "RCA has the equipment that will be used and we have the books."[9] In fact, the structure and objectives of nontext product development have generally followed the lines of text development.

The experience of one firm, considered to be a pioneer in the nontext field, is illustrative. When the firm first entered the audiovisual materials market, it conducted product development in a special audiovisual department structured differently from the standard text development department. This structure soon evolved so that a staff specialist in audiovisual techniques worked with editors and authors; this structure in turn "evolved into an integrated team approach in which the specialist has virtually disappeared."[10] The department's structure approached that of the text editorial department, with the "project editor" or "project manager" the counterpart of the supervising editor. The department's evolving objectives similarly centered on marketing needs. "The first step" in product development "is a written product definition, which in effect is a first attempt at the sales catalogue copy."[11]

A 1969 study of sixty-five firms in the instructional materials industry, conducted by the Institute for Educational Development (IED), confirms this view.[12] The affiliation of electronics and publishing firms in the 1960s promised the transfer of research and development methods and findings from one to the other, but these transfers have not in fact materialized. To be sure, respondents from the four subsidiaries of electronics firms sampled in the study consistently asserted that they used their parent's research in their own product improvement. Actually, corporate parents, both electronics and broadcasting firms, have been repeatedly frustrated in their efforts to transfer their own research and development styles to acquired subsidiaries. Apparently only a slightly greater degree of success has been enjoyed in the attempts to transfer these styles to company divisions.

All six of the independent nontext producers canvassed in the IED study generally appeared to conform their research and development practices to the incremental approach taken by textbook publishers. Two of the six did, however, indicate a more structured concern for market research and field testing than is common among textbook publishers. And of the five canvassed nontext producers that are subsidiaries or divisions of text publishing firms, all but one appeared to embrace the textbook model of incremental development, although here too concern for field testing of materials was at least more explicit.

The direct evidence on product development in the instructional materials industry is sparse and largely anecdotal. Yet it does begin to confirm a point already suggested by the more complete facts on patterns of consumer demand. Research and development in this industry in fact consists of product development aimed at slight differentiation rather than at major instructional objectives.

This conclusion is also confirmed by some theoretical implications that can be drawn from a snapshot of firms, structure, and competition in the instructional materials industry.

Snapshot of an Industry

Approximately eighty firms publish textbooks for grades K–8. Some of these firms are also among the more than one hundred that produce nontext instructional materials for the K–8 market.[13] Many of these firms produce instructional materials for the high school and college markets. Some also engage in general publishing, and some in the production of instructional materials for military and industrial uses. These overlaps make it difficult to assemble comparable data definitively portraying sales, firm size, and structure in the K–8 instructional materials industry, but some broad contours can be suggested.

In 1971, the best recent year for comparing data, sales of instructional materials for grades K–8 amounted to $424,040,000. Sales of texts and standardized tests accounted for about three-quarters of this total, or $314,040,000.[14] The other one-quarter, $110,000,000, was derived from sales of audiovisual materials, including films, filmstrips, slides, recorders, tapes and multimedia kits.[15] Text and test sales for K–8 represented roughly 35 percent of total text and test sales at all levels, elementary through college, and 10 percent of total book publishing industry sales in 1971. Audiovisual materials sales for K–8 represented roughly 57 percent of total revenues derived from audiovisual sales to all grade levels that year.

Firm Size

Against the scale of operations maintained by America's major industrial corporations, sales by firms in the instructional materials industry appear small. Among the twenty largest firms in the industry, annual revenues for elhi text and audiovisual materials producers range from $97 million for the largest to $12 million for the twentieth-largest. Average annual revenues among the top twenty are $40 million.[16] Numbers of employees are not available for the instructional materials industry, but 1967 data on employee distribution in the more generally defined publishing industry are suggestive. Of 1,022 establishments listed, only one had over 2,500 employees, eight had between 1,000 and 2,499 and ten between 500 and 999.[17]

At first glance, firm size might be cause for pessimism about the prospects for significant research and development expenditures, because there is some evidence that large firms invest more in research and development as a fraction of total revenues than do smaller firms. Comparative investment figures for

1969, for example, reveal that firms with over 5,000 employees committed, on the average, 5.2 percent of sales to research and development; those with between 1,000 and 5,000 employees averaged 2.2 percent; those with less than 1,000 employees, 2.0 percent.[18]

Yet it is easy to overstate the point that in research and development big is best. Research and development consists roughly of three discrete steps—articulation of a basic concept, development of the concept into a workable form, and modification of the working model to meet commercial needs. Typically, each step involves the commitment of more resources than the preceding one. Although all three steps might be carried out in the large, resourceful firm, the first, least costly, step might just as easily be taken by a small firm, bringing its invention to a threshold at which patent or other protection can be obtained and beyond which venture capital financing can be secured or a large firm induced to carry on the development over the last two stages.[19]

The development of nylon by Dupont is illustrative.[20] The total expense of the efforts leading to nylon's production has been placed at $10,560,000. Yet the presumably patentable process for making nylon had been reached in the first stage of development, involving an outlay estimated at only $787,000. Had it been a small, modestly financed inventor who had conceived the process, he or she might have sold the discovery to Dupont or some other large firm for development, or might have sought venture capital financing to develop it independently.

The development of nylon illustrates another important point about research and development in small firms of the sort that make up the instructional materials industry. Dr. Wallace Carothers, the inventor of the process for producing nylon, was not hired by Dupont to discover or develop this particular process, but rather to conduct basic research without regard for its commercial value. In the course of Carother's scientific inquiries, he made the serendipitous discovery that led to nylon's development. Yet small firms are not inclined to conduct basic research. The principal reason for this is that although development costs are relatively low at the first stages and the outcomes relatively predictable, the basic research that precedes the first stages typically involves high costs and yields few predictable outcomes. Often these outcomes are in the form of basic scientific precepts that are not in themselves patentable. With low costs and good prospects of financing or licensing under its patent, the small firm as well as the large one will be attracted to the first stages of development. Because the unpredictable outcomes of basic research may bear no relationship to any single production activity in which the firm is engaged, it is the large, relatively diversified firm that will more likely be attracted to this enterprise.

All of these points are quite general and do not uniformly apply to conditions in the instructional materials industry. For example, because some elements of investment are not proportionately as costly as they are in other industries, considerations of scale may be less important than usual. Prototypes can be produced relatively cheaply, for there is rarely a need to fabricate new production equipment. The classroom, not the development laboratory, is the site for much product testing. Participation by students and evaluation by teachers mean that experimentation costs to the producer will be comparatively low, in effect subsidized by school systems. Also, measuring firm size against such standard benchmarks as number of employees may well understate the industry's commitment to research and development. A greater proportion of the employees in any instructional materials firm will be directly or indirectly involved in research and development than in many other industries. Editors, writers, and sales personnel are all in some ways a part of the research and development process.

Concentration, Competition and Entry

Concentration ratios compare the revenues of the largest firms in an industry to the industry's overall revenues. As an index of market structure, concentration ratios may shed some light on the behavior of firms in the industry and specifically on firms' propensity to invest in research and development. Where a single firm is responsible for all industry revenues (a 1:1 ratio), monopoly exists. Where no single firm or handful of firms possess a significant market share, the market is competitive. And where, as is typical, the concentration ratio lies somewhere in between, a mix of monopoly and competitive behavior can be expected.

None of the available industry concentration ratios precisely fits the K–8 market, but two sources do provide some guidance. The single most relevant class in the Census Bureau's *Concentration Ratios in Manufacturing* is "Text books including teacher's editions," and includes high school and college, along with elementary, texts, but excludes audiovisual and programmed instruction materials. According to the 1967 figures, 29 percent of the value of shipments in this class was accounted for by the four largest companies. The eight largest companies accounted for 50 percent, the twenty largest for 79 percent, and the fifty largest for 94 percent.[21] These 1967 textbook figures are roughly paralleled by figures compiled by Knowledge Industry Publications for 1972 sales of all instructional materials, text and nontext, for the elementary through high school grades. In that year the four largest firms accounted for 32 percent of sales, the eight largest for 53 percent, and the twenty largest for 75 percent. An earlier report, for 1970 sales, showed the four largest companies to have a 27 percent market share and the eight largest, 47 percent.[22]

Although there were shifts in position among the top ten firms between 1970 and 1973, there were no new entrants to their ranks. Yet entry and exit among the remaining firms appear to be relatively fluid. The level at which scale economies arise is far less clear. One survey of the industry asserts that there "are distinct economies of scale in the educational materials industry. . . . Selling textbooks and other materials requires a national marketing effort, involving some combination of direct selling, direct mail and space advertising"; the same survey elsewhere reveals that among the major text and audiovisual producers, sales staffs vary in size from five to 175.[23] Indeed, it is probably inaccurate to speak of scale economies in publishing, because a firm can contract out all major functions—distribution, production, and even editing.

Some entry barriers may be posed by state adoption systems under which state rather than local agencies select the materials to be used throughout the state. These systems often require participating publishers to demonstrate an established level of experience, resources and financial stability. They may erect additional barriers through the exclusionary effects of the contracts awarded, ranging from three to seven years in duration. Yet in at least one state, California, several small firms that produce almost exclusively for the California market appear to have thrived under an adoption regime. Furthermore, the contemporary shift from adoption systems to systems under which local districts assume responsibility for materials selection, suggests that these barriers, if they exist, are quickly falling.

One factor that might affect conditions of both entry and concentration is patterns of acquisition and merger. Since the post-Sputnik flurry of activity, industry history has been marked by the entry of large communications firms into educational publishing through mergers or acquisitions. Among some of the more widely noted combinations are the 1962 joint venture by General Electric and Time, Inc., to form General Learning Corp.; IBM's purchase in 1969 of Science Research Associates; RCA's 1966 acquisition of Random House; CBS's merger with Holt, Rinehart and Winston in 1967; and Xerox's 1962 merger with Ginn and Company. Whatever their success, these mergers and acquisitions probably did not lead to increased industry concentration, for while sales of merged or acquired companies increased, so did industry sales overall.

In theory, the moderate degrees of concentration and the relative ease of entry that prevail in the instructional materials industry suggest that the industry leaders, because they compete, will seek to outdo each other in making their goods attractive to consumers. Because they realize that their behavior and that of their rivals are interdependent, they will tend to shun self-defeating forms of competition, such as price competition. Instead they will engage in forms of competition less easily countered by their rivals and better calculated to confer competitive advantage. Competitive product differentiation is one characteristic form of behavior in these circumstances.

In fact, competition in the instructional materials industry does appear to center on quality as well as price. According to one source, the pricing of elhi texts is somewhat closer than it is for college texts, but price cutting is not actively pursued. Though sensitive to the cost-consciousness of text selection boards, publishers also invest in and stress the qualitative differences in their products, through attempts at more attractive presentation of material, more frequent issuance of revised editions, and distribution of complimentary teaching guides and other aids to instruction.[24]

Size, Structure and Incentives to Invent

Conditions in the instructional materials industry are consistent with low levels of investment aimed at sufficient product differentiation to avoid charges of copyright infringement. Yet these conditions are not inconsistent with sharply increased investment in research and development aimed at more dramatic objectives. But before such change can occur, schools will have to shift their demands toward more dramatic objectives. Also, more effective legal mechanisms for protecting research and development will have to become available, whether in conjunction with direct subsidy programs or not.

Some investment patterns observed in the pharmaceuticals industry several years ago may help to illustrate the implications of market structure and legal mechanisms for investment in invention.[25] At the time of these observations, the pharmaceuticals industry was, like the instructional materials industry, moderately concentrated, consisting of a few large firms and many small firms. Competition centered on factors other than price, usually product differentiation.

Unlike the instructional materials industry, however, the pharmaceuticals industry was divided into discrete, highly concentrated submarkets. "In a group of twenty such markets," for example, "the proportion of output accounted for by the leading five firms ranged from 56 percent to 98 percent." To some extent these concentration levels were maintained by high promotional expenditures. To a more significant extent, it was research and development expenditures, and resulting collections of patents, that sustained this structure.

Patent law is the primary vehicle for protecting the results of pharmaceutical research and development, both new products and new manufacturing processes. Research and development must be more than modestly focused if the outcomes are to be sufficiently inventive to qualify under the patent law's exacting standards of nonobviousness and novelty. Consequently, firms seeking to enter any patent-dominated submarket face the costs of substantial research and development efforts unless firms already in the submarket will license their patents to outsiders. These costs will be encountered regardless of whether the newcomer seeks patent protection for its own products, for the firm must, to compete, sufficiently differentiate its products from those of entrenched firms to escape claims of patent infringement.

Copyright rather than patent protection dominates the instructional materials industry. Copyright requires a far lower degree of product differentiation for protection to be obtained or infringement avoided. The levels of research and development investment and the barriers surrounding submarkets are correspondingly low. This suggests that if copyright protection is augmented by more rigorous forms of protection for instructional materials, and if altered school structures begin to demand more of instructional materials, increased levels of invention should result. The industry's competitive structure could also change.

Intellectual Properties in the Instructional Marketplace

Copyright, patent, and trade secret law are commonly called intellectual properties to distinguish them from their age-old counterparts, real and personal property, and to suggest their dominion over creations of the mind. Each in its own way seeks to resolve the problems of inappropriability that deter firms from investing in research and development. Essentially, the means employed is a government promise to all who privately undertake research and development that they will enjoy a legal monopoly over their newly developed subject matter for a specified period. By granting the originator an exclusive right to profit from its creation, the intellectual properties are thought to induce investment in research and development that might otherwise not occur.

Because these legal nets are cast over information, rather than realty or personalty, courts have been particularly alert to perceived untoward extensions of the monopoly. In the case of copyright, the motive may lie in first amendment traditions against restraints on speech or press. In the case of patent law, the explicit concern has been use of the patent monopoly to obtain excessive market power. In both cases, and less explicitly in trade secret law, there is a clear antipathy to the use of these mechanisms for monopolizing ideas. "Surely," one scholar has noted, "it would be intolerable to give a patent on most of the fundamental ideas that arise from basic research."[26]

To withhold protection from basic ideas is of course to withhold incentive for private investment to produce them. In copyright law, incentive is withheld under the law's governing principle that protection will be extended to expressions, but not to their underlying ideas. Patent law does not protect "fundamental ideas," but it does protect those that are considered less basic. The patent system might for this reason appear to offer some inducement to investment in ideas by instructional materials producers. The reason that patent law does not occupy an important place in instructional materials development lies in another quarter—its refusal to protect subject matter that expressly depends for its utility upon interaction with the human mind. Finally, trade secret law, though it may offer some protection to instructional materials producers, suffers special limitations of its own.

Copyright

As the legal system most broadly associated with the production of instructional materials, copyright bears some responsibility for the fact that product development aims to produce instructional materials that differ from one another in expression and appearance but not in their underlying ideas. The idea-expression distinction is chiefly responsible. For the producer of instructional materials, the division between unprotectable ideas and protectable expressions means that there will be scant inducement to invest in research and development of new instructional techniques—essentially, ideas—the value of which could be quickly and freely appropriated by competitors.

There are, of course, other systems of incentive to invest in ideas, and copyright may have a role to play in implementing these systems. Federally supported research programs often include copyright licensing policies under which publishers are licensed to produce materials embodying the research results. But to the extent that development costs must be incurred to make the idea workable in the context of a program or text series, and to the extent that marketing efforts must be undertaken to gain consumer acceptance for the new idea, copyright cannot be expected to serve as the vehicle for recovering development and marketing expenditures.

Ideas and Expressions. *Baker v. Selden*,[27] decided by the United States Supreme Court in 1879, illustrates the distinction between ideas and their expression. The case involved a claim that the plaintiff's copyright in the book *Selden's Condensed Ledger, or Book-keeping Simplified* had been infringed by Baker's work. The plaintiff's book consisted of "an introductory essay explaining the system of bookkeeping referred to, to which are annexed certain forms or blanks, consisting of ruled lines, and headings, illustrating the system and showing how it is to be used and carried out in practice." The defendant's work was comparable, using "a similar plan so far as results are concerned," but with a different arrangement of the columns and different headings. Apparently Baker did not copy the introductory essay to Selden's book.

The Supreme Court rested its decision for the defendant on the view that where methods or techniques such as bookkeeping are involved, copyright extends only to the arrangement of words used by the author to explain his method, and not to the underlying method itself. Baker may have borrowed Selden's system, but no copyright action could lie for the taking. Had Baker copied the introductory essay rather than the method of arranging columns, an action for infringement would have been made out. Had he instead rephrased the essay, using its underlying ideas but not its expression, he would not have been liable.

In its differentiation between the protected and unprotected elements of the Selden treatise, the Court made clear that it was applying no more than copyright law's traditional division between protectable expressions and their informing, unprotectable ideas. Where, like ideas generally, "the truths of a science or the methods of an art are the common property of the whole world, any author has the right to express the one, or explain or use the other, in his own way." In a subsequent passage, the Court provided a distinctive rationale for its adherence to the traditional position. Ideas, the Court reasoned, are "common property," not because they may be old or otherwise not original to an author but rather because, as ideas, they are too important to be monopolized through copyright.

Baker v. Selden spawned two lines of decision that are immediately relevant to instructional materials. One line of decision holds that blank forms designed for recording information cannot be copyrighted. Account books, charts, scorecards, and report forms are the typical subjects of these decisions.[28] In one case, for example, a court found plaintiff's calibrated graphic charts uncopyrightable on the ground that, like the bookkeeping forms in *Baker v. Selden*, the chart forms were not intended to communicate facts or ideas, but only to record facts.[29]

Other courts have escaped the rule, not by attacking it, but simply by assuming the rule's validity and holding that the particular form before it conveyed the requisite information.[30] Thus, in *Harcourt, Brace & World, Inc. v. Graphic Controls Corp.*,[31] the court rejected the accused infringer's argument that the plaintiff's printed answer sheets, designed for use in conjunction with student achievement and intelligence tests and for correction by optical scanners, "are not a proper subject for copyright under the rule of *Baker v. Selden* . . . because their format is fixed by the requirements of the optical scanning machine. . . ." Recognizing that "the area for originality of design is limited by the requirements of the optical scanning machine used," the court concluded that the answer sheets conveyed the necessary amount of information. "On their face they inform a reader that they are designed to be the page upon which one records responses to an examination in a certain way; explanations and examples appear in the design of some answer sheets."

A second line of authority that has evolved from *Baker v. Selden* consists of cases in which the nature of the idea prevents it from being expressed in more than a small number of ways. One case involved the copyrightability of contest rules which required "if not only one form of expression at best only a limited number." To allow copyright over these rules, the court held, would mean that "a party or parties, by copyrighting a mere handful of forms, could exhaust all possibilities of future use of the substance."[32] Conceding the distinction between uncopyrightable ideas and copyrightable expression, courts in these cases held expression to be unprotectable on the ground that to protect it would improperly extend a monopoly over the underlying idea.

In another case involving several insurance instruments and related legal forms, the court rested its decision that there had been no infringement on the observation that "in the fields of insurance and commerce the use of specific language in forms and documents may be so essential to accomplish a desired result and so integrated with the use of a legal or commercial conception that the proper standard of infringement is one which will protect as far as possible the copyrighted language and yet allow free use of the thought beneath the language."[33]

Under the first line of cases, disqualification of subject matter designed to record but not to convey information probably has only a limited effect on investment in instructional materials research and development. From the viewpoint of copyright doctrine, the fault with blank forms is not that they record rather than convey information, but rather that their own information is so sparse and inexpressive. To be useful, programs will generally be informative. Copyright will withhold its inducement only from the design of dependent elements of a program—worksheets, perhaps, or forms for recording answers or scores.

The effect of the second line of cases, barring protection for expressions that vary only narrowly from their underlying ideas, may be somewhat more significant. The fault with expressions that do little more than echo their underlying idea is not so much that the number of expressions of the idea is limited but rather that to extend protection to the expression will curtail competition in the idea. Firms will be dissuaded from developing ideas whose utility, they expect, will depend upon their precise formulation in a limited number of ways.

Another consequence of the idea-expression distinction may be more important to investment behavior. Because the law forbids copying a copyright proprietor's expression, competitors are legally compelled to introduce products that embody expressive differences from the originator's work. But given the lack of protection for ideas and investment in them, these differences will be relatively minimal. Thus the marketplace for instructional materials will, to the extent that competition exists, be crowded with works that, though different in their expressions, are essentially redundant in their ideas.[34] In the case of works of fiction, where expression rather than idea is chiefly valued, this result may be viewed as desirable. Where, as is presumably the case with instructional materials, efficiency, not aesthetics, is the objective, there may be some cause for concern that copyright law compels as a condition of doing business that investment be directed to marginally different expressions of the same idea.

Educational Uses. Withholding protection for ideas is only one of the ways in which copyright limits incentives to invest in instructional programs. Another problem is the fair use doctrine, which exempts educational uses of copyrighted works from liability under certain circumstances. The reasoning behind educational exemptions is that, because they are engaged in a worthy and eleemosynary enterprise, educational users deserve to enjoy free that for which other users must pay. These views appeared frequently in the hearings held in connection with contemporary efforts to revise the 1909 Copyright Act. One prominent group of instructional materials users, the Ad Hoc Committee (of Educational Institutions and Organizations) on Copyright Law Revision, proposed that the revision bill's fair-use provision be augmented by a separate exemption specially tailored to fit the needs of educational users and specifically providing that "nonprofit use of a portion of a copyrighted work for noncommercial teaching, scholarship or research is not an infringement of copyright." To justify its proposal the committee held that educational users "do not use materials for their own gain but for the benefit of the children of all of our citizens, including those of authors and publishers."[35]

Of course, the price must be paid somewhere. Generally it is paid in the form of implicit subsidies coming from other, noneducational users and lowered investment in the development of materials for educational markets. The effects of this exemption will be particularly severe for instructional materials, where the schoolroom usually represents the producer's primary market, so that other, noneducational uses do not substantially subsidize exempted educational uses.

Long the subject of evolving definition by judicial decision, the fair-use doctrine was eventually committed to statutory form in section 107 of the 1976 Copyright Act, excusing "the fair use of a copyrighted work" for "purposes such as criticism, comment, news reporting, teaching, scholarship or research."[36] Section 107 charts no new course for fair use and embodies principles that have informed the doctrine from its beginnings. Among the factors to be considered in determining the fairness of a particular use are "the nature of the copyrighted work," "the amount and substantiality of the portion used," and "the effect of the use upon the potential market for or value of the copyrighted work."

Williams & Wilkins Co. v. United States[37] suggests some of the long-run implications of fair-use doctrine for instructional materials research and development. Under the facts of *Williams & Wilkins*, the plaintiff, a medical publisher serving physicians, schools, and libraries, charged that two federal research institutions, the National Institute of Health and the National Library of Medicine, had infringed several of its copyrights by photocopying articles from its journals for distribution inside and outside the two facilities. At issue was whether the photocopying constituted copyright infringement or was to be excused as fair use on the ground that the photocopying was done by government agencies for research purposes.

The trial judge ruled that infringement had been made out. The Court of Claims reversed, resting its ruling on three propositions, the first of which was that plaintiff had not shown that it was being substantially harmed by the activities of the two research institutions. Unable to muster a majority on either side of the question, the Supreme Court divided 4-4, thus effectively if not authoritatively affirming the Court of Claims decision for defendant.

The Court of Claims' first proposition, that "Plaintiff has not in our view shown ... that it is being or will be harmed substantially by these specific practices," forms the linchpin of fair-use doctrine. Unfortunately, the proposition rests upon a highly artificial view of copyright markets. When a teacher reproduces brief passages from a publisher's book, the doctrine excuses the activity on the ground that the publisher is not himself in the business of printing and selling such brief passages and so is not harmed. Yet, there is no reason, apart from the operation of fair-use doctrine, why the publisher could not enter this reprint market. A teacher's reproduction of parts of a text through photocopying, of parts of an audiovisual program through audio and video cassette recording, or of elements of a kit through reconstruction with devices purchased at the five-and-dime, are all activities in which the copyright proprietor could himself engage or, more likely, license others specializing in this sort of production to pursue.

The further problem with the proposition is that harm, in the sense supposed, plays no role in the pricing behavior of copyright proprietors. A publisher who is unable to exact revenues from one class of users, photocopiers, will not himself suffer harm or attempt to subsidize publication, but will attempt to recoup his production costs from levies on other classes—in the case of Williams & Wilkins, subscribers. The producer naturally runs the risk of driving subscribers to nonpaying uses such as library photocopying; as a result, to maintain product quality, subscription prices will have to be set still higher for the remaining subscribers, probably libraries in this case.

These steps can in turn be expected to lead to either or both of two results. The direction of the producer's investment in product development will increasingly be narrowed to meet the interests of the narrowing class of subscribers, possibly diverging from the interests of the wider class of the product's users. Where a school board purchases a small number of copies of materials and freely permits their photocopying by teachers, the materials producer will be deprived of important information about the utility of its materials to teachers and students. One instructional program may be copied hundreds of times within a district, another only a handful of times. Because the same number of programs was originally sold for each, the instructional materials producer will have only limited access to the sort of information that producers generally rely on in determining the appropriate direction for investment in new products.

Second, reduction in the number of consumers may lead to reductions in the level of investment in product development. A loss of sales to one group of consumers means higher prices to the remainder if the level of investment in product development is to be maintained. Conceivably, some boards will be willing to pay the higher price, seeing this as a far more efficient way to spend the money than the purchase of many more copies of texts and other materials than will ever be used. Yet at some point, as the price of instructional materials increases, school boards may begin to look for less expensive substitutes, such as children's books prepared for more general markets, or increased use of teachers or teaching assistants. At this point the instructional materials producer will reduce his investment in product development to remain competitive.

Patent Law

Copyright decisions like *Baker v. Selden*, which withhold protection from ideas and methods, frequently point to patent law as the appropriate vehicle for protection of the kind being sought. While patent law does protect ideas and methods more than does copyright law, its subject matter is also circumscribed. Indeed, Selden's bookkeeping system would have failed to qualify for patent protection on two grounds. Because the system closely tracked basic book-keeping principles, it would have been disqualified from patent protection under the natural principles exclusion. Because the system necessarily relied on human participation to achieve its purpose, it would also have been disqualified under the mental process exception.

Both these exclusionary grounds are relevant to the protection of instructional materials. Because of the natural principles exclusion, publishers have no patent incentive to discover fundamental learning patterns or to develop materials framed transparently around these patterns, old or new. The implications of the mental process exclusion are still more serious. By their very nature, instructional materials depend upon student participation and reaction, and if this exception is rigorously applied, no instructional program would qualify for protection.

Natural Principles. Long neglected by the courts, the natural principles exclusion was recently revived by the United States Supreme Court in *Gottschalk v. Benson*.[38] The Court there applied the doctrine to hold that a method for converting binary-coded decimal numerals into binary form for use in a general purpose digital computer was unpatentable. Stating the question for decision to be "whether the method described and claimed is a 'process' within the meaning of the Patent Act," the Court rested its negative answer on the view that "phenomena of nature, though just discovered, mental processes, and abstract intellectual concepts are not patentable, as they are the basic tools of scientific and technological work."

The asserted danger of giving patent protection to natural principles is the stultifying effect that this would have on the research efforts of others. The substance of this fear was well expressed in a decision rendered over a century earlier, *O'Reilly v. Morse*, invalidating the eighth claim of Samuel Morse's telegraphy patent for "use of the motive power of the electric or galvanic current . . . for marking or printing intelligible characters, signs, or letters at any distances. . . ." To validate this claim, the Court declared, would not only enable Morse to shut the door against invention by others but would also put him in a position "to avail himself of new discoveries in the properties and powers of electro-magnetism which scientific men might bring to light."[39]

The natural principles rule has one significant limitation. When the subject matter in question represents a major, pioneer invention, courts have been less inclined to invalidate claims that hardly do more than mirror their underlying natural principles. In the *Telephone Cases*, the Court rejected a charge made by alleged infringers of the Bell telephone patent that the patent impermissibly covered the natural principles governing the use of electricity for the transmission of sound.[40] The Court recognized that "It may be that electricity cannot be used at all for the transmission of speech except in the way Bell has discovered and that therefore practically, his patent gives him an exclusive use for that purpose." But it concluded, "that does not make his claim one for the use of electricity distinct from the particular process with which it is connected in his patent. It will, if true, show more clearly the great importance of his discovery but it will not invalidate his patent."

One consequence of the natural principles rule is to divert private investment away from research into basic principles of learning behavior and toward the development of materials incorporating known principles. Although the rule applies to research and development in all fields, its application seems particularly debilitating for instructional materials. The body of behavioral precepts underlying instructional materials is far less developed than the bodies of scientific principle, like chemistry and physics, on which other fields of applied research are based. Only if directly subsidized research efforts begin to fill this vacuum with fundamental scientific discoveries might the patent law begin to attract investment in the development of products incorporating them.

Mental Processes. Patent law requires the patentee to reduce patented subject matter to terms from which anyone skilled in the relevant art can recreate it exactly. The reasons for the requirement are that, during the patent term the patent should be sufficiently instructive to enable research by others, and that upon the patent's expiration, it should convey sufficient information to enable competitors to reproduce and improve it. Where the patent subject matter relies upon human participation for its operation, this reliance is frequently thought to impede reproduction. Consequently, patents have been denied where the claimed subject matter was either intended to affect human behavior or depended for its operation on human intervention.

Ex parte Mayne[41] is an example of unpatentability on the ground that subject matter affects human behavior. The applicant's claims for a method of combating seasickness "and causing the person voluntarily to manifest his apprehension thereof" were rejected on the ground that the "term 'causing' here is deemed inapt for the manifestation of apprehension is purely a mental effect." The thrust of these decisions has not seriously been challenged and has apparently been accepted by even the most severe critics of the mental process doctrine. No principle has been offered, however, to distinguish these cases from those involving areas such as medical technology, where effects are similarly "mental" or physical, but where patentability is nonetheless assumed.

Johnson v. Duquesne Light Co.[42] involved a process that depended upon human activity for its execution rather than its effect. The subject matter there, "a method of testing strings of suspension insulators in live transmission wires" was rejected because the "lineman making the test must know from experience about what the normal voltage distribution is over the different insulators of the string." The court gave as the reason for rejection that the claims in suit did not "prescribe a method which, if followed, will produce a certain result." The claims were disallowed "because they produce no results proceeding directly from the operation of the theory or plan laid down in the claims. To be patentable, a method laid down to be followed must produce the desired result from the mere following of the method prescribed."

One special rule is concerned with products that, through their incorporation of printed matter, necessarily implicate mental activity. Essentially, the rule holds that a patent will not be granted for articles of manufacture whose only advance over the prior art lies in the significance of the printed matter appearing on them. In *Ex parte Gwin*,[43] a patent was withheld from applicant's parlor golf game, which employed dice bearing the usual dots but with some variations in spacing and colors. The ground given was that the "*sole* difference over the art is in the printed matter," the indicia on the dice. Under the rule adopted in the case, the instructions or techniques conveyed by the printed matter, however novel and inventive, will not support valid claims unless the underlying article or the juxtaposition of printed matter on the article is independently patentable. And in either case the claim must be directed to the article or the new structural relation, not to the printed matter itself.

There is of course a fine, sometimes indistinguishable line between printed matter alone and printed matter in a new structural relation. The modern trend has been to draw the line in favor of patentability by construing "structural relation" broadly or by substituting other relations for structural ones. The rationale of one early case, *Cincinnati Traction Co. v. Pope*,[44] has been used to expand the concept of structural relation. The court there held that the arrangement of printed matter on a streetcar ticket transfer constituted a new and patentable structural relation. In a recent case, where novel placement of indicia on measuring cups and spoons was claimed, "functional" rather than "structural" relation was looked to in order to find patentability.[45] And in a still more recent case involving an answer sheet for use in self-instruction and testing, the charge of nonpatentability on the ground of printed matter was tersely and opaquely dismissed. "This is not a valid reason for rejection," the court declared. "Printed matter may very well constitute structural limitations upon which patentability can be predicated."[46]

The printed matter exception is just one instance of the absence of the patent incentive from instructional materials research and development. Rules withholding protection from mental processes have special force in an area where research is specifically focused on the factors governing learning behavior and where products necessarily entail human effects and intervention. To be sure, these rules do not entirely exclude protection for this class of subject matter, but they offer little inducement to private development of new instructional techniques.

The effects of the rule excluding protection for subject matter directed toward modification of intellectual behavior is important, for useful instructional materials must by nature alter student behavior. The one possible qualification to this rule, permitting a patent where the mental effects can be explained and predicted according to some theoretical framework, has little bearing on instructional materials, as no integrated theory of learning is available to serve that purpose. At the same time, state-mandated programs of learner verification for instructional materials, though motivated by other considerations, may contribute to the development of the needed empirical and theoretical base.

Trade Secrets

Even without copyright, patent or other special inducement, firms commit some resources to research and development in new and improved products. The lure is the goodwill and profits to be derived during the period between the originator's introduction of his product and the appearance of his competitor's copies. If the originator can extend this period by secreting the inventive elements of his product, he will enjoy an even stronger inducement. Critics of the copyright and patent systems cite this "lead time" phenomenon to support their position that research and development will be conducted for new and better products even without copyright and patent protection.

Although secrecy may protect some investment in instructional materials research and development, investment will clearly be directed toward the development of subject matter intrinsically easy to keep secret, and away from information whose embodiments will be self-revealing or readily reverse engineered. The shelter of secrecy would also appear to stimulate investment in incremental more than in major innovation. Major innovations, to the extent that they attract added profits, will also attract competitors more readily disposed to incur the costs of uncovering secret information.

A recently decided case, *SmokEnders, Inc. v. Smoke No More, Inc.*[47] provides a helpful introduction to issues in this area. The plaintiff had devoted substantial effort to developing a program for instructing individuals in how to give up smoking. The scheme, "a step-by-step regimented program which requires that each person attending a SE [SmokEnders] program perform each element of the program at a particular time," was formalized in a 170-page manual, adhered to closely by plaintiff's "moderators" as they administered the program to participants. Among the elaborate precautions taken by SmokEnders to maintain the secrecy of its program and manual was a requirement that program participants agree in writing that they would not disclose any portion of the program. Participants were not permitted access to the manual.

The court ruled that the "SE program is a trade secret in that it is (1) the product of many hours of labor, (2) of commercial value to competitors, (3) could only be prepared by competitors at great expense, (4) has been kept secret by agreement and complexity of the program, and (5) is novel." It concluded that defendants, former SmokEnders employees, had unlawfully exploited SmokEnders's program in their own competing course.

The program involved in *SmokEnders* has many of the characteristics of instructional materials and programs generally, and the case highlights some of the conditions, legal and nonlegal, that surround investment in instructional materials. Specifically, the case underscores the distinction between a firm's ability to appropriate the value of a program on its own, through informal mechanisms such as secrecy and loyalty, and a firm's need to rely on legal mechanisms other than copyright and patent—in this case, trade secret law. As will be seen, the prevailing nonlegal mechanisms, at least in the context of instructional materials, are weak at best and provide little inducement to investment in research and development. As will also be seen, the legal trade secret mechanism is characteristically flaccid. Trade secret law as customarily applied exerts a far less powerful lure to investment in new ideas than does the patent law, and possibly even less than the copyright law.

Secrecy. It is far easier for a firm to secrete information about its processes than information embodied in its products. A process, such as a way of binding a book more effectively and at lower cost, may be fully performed within the firm's plant, often by a small number of employees. On the other hand, vital information embodied in the product itself is open to public examination, so it is difficult to keep the underlying information secret. This is particularly so when, as in *SmokEnders* and in the case of instructional materials generally, the product *is* information.

A typical audience for instructional materials will be much larger and better informed than the audience that effectively destroyed secrecy under the facts of *SmokEnders*. Publishers' sales representatives can be expected to familiarize themselves with their product's method of operation at least as thoroughly as did the "moderators" employed by SmokEnders. Purchasing officials and teachers will demand to know the full details of a program's concept and method to judge its efficacy. Instructional materials are bought in quantity and by purchasers with relatively more expertise than the purchaser of consumer goods and services. As a result there is greater opportunity and more pressure to inspect the goods before purchase.

Law. Lead time is not the only way to secure the values of invention. Legal mechanisms can also be used to enforce the bonds of secrecy that loyalty and good faith alone will not tie. This was presumably the motive behind the secrecy agreements that SmokEnders extracted from its employees and program participants. Trade secret law might appear to offer a commodious shelter for the protection of new ideas. It prohibits the unauthorized use of information disclosed in confidence or obtained by improper means, such as theft. Unlike copyright law, trade secret law protects ideas. Unlike patent law, it imposes no formal qualitative standards. Consequently, a wide variety of technical and nontechnical developments, even customer lists and promotional strategies, may qualify for protection.

In fact, the operational scope of trade secret law is far less ambitious than it appears. For an infringement action to lie, the subject matter in dispute must meet some standards. It must be a "formula, pattern, device or compilation of information which is used in one's business, and which gives him an opportunity to obtain an advantage over competitors who do not know or use it." For a taking of the secret to be actionable, it must have been accomplished either through breach of confidence or some other improper means, such as "fraudulent misrepresentations to induce disclosure" or "tapping of telephone wires, eavesdropping or other espionage."[48] Secrecy must not only be rigorously proven, but it must also be shown that the information being used by the defendant was the plaintiff's secret and that it was improperly obtained. If the plaintiff's information borders on common knowledge or on knowledge easily replicable from public domain sources, and if the defendant arrived at the information through independent efforts, such as analysis of the plaintiff's product, protection is foreclosed.

Also, practical obstacles stand in the way of the law's guarantee of secrecy. Litigation necessarily entails the disclosure of the plaintiff's secret and, often, his surrounding business and research and development practices as well. A protective order can restrict disclosure to the defendant's attorneys, but the exigencies of suit necessarily limit such an order's effect. The chance that more advantage will be lost by suing than by not suing exerts a powerful disincentive to pursuit of the legal remedy. Criminal prosecutions are few, in part because of the extremely narrow formulation of the conduct proscribed. Where the action is against a departing employee, as is most frequently the case, problems of proof are compounded by limits on the extent to which courts will allow employee mobility to be restrained through trade secret injunctions or covenants not to compete.

After all this, the most that the trade secret claimant can hope to gain from a lawsuit is to have the defendant placed in the position he would have occupied had he acted lawfully. Compensatory damages are the rule, attorneys' fees and punitive damages the exception. As a result, the plaintiff's head start will usually be monetized. Under the generally applicable rule, an injunction will run for only so long as the trade secret remains secret, and will be dissolved when the protected information enters the public domain, through widespread reverse engineering, independent discovery or the issuance of a patent.

The Need for Private Incentives

Educational publishers will not invest in the development of inventive instructional ideas because they know that schools generally will resist innovation. Yet, other factors make publishers reluctant to invest in instructional materials research and development, and these will demand attention if school systems someday become more innovative. One such cause is the lack of any substantial incentives to invention in the form of intellectual property. A related cause is the structure of the instructional materials industry and the size of its firms. Thus, as hard as it will be to accomplish, the reform of American schools will not be sufficient to increase investment in instructional materials research and development. Revisions in private systems of incentive will also be needed, at least so long as private industry continues to be the main supplier of the nation's instructional materials.

5

Subsidies to Innovation in Instructional Materials

Subsidies are employed today to stimulate activity at all stages of instructional materials research and development, from an idea's genesis through its embodiment in a product used by schoolchildren. As seen in chapter 3, school systems have many reasons not to adopt inventive instructional materials. And even apart from consumer indifference, producers enjoy few incentives to perform basic research or to develop findings into significantly inventive products, essentially for the reasons explored in chapter 4. The main object of subsidies is to cut through these patterns of producer and consumer indifference.

A series of grants from the National Science Foundation supported *Science—A Process Approach*, enabling the American Association for the Advancement of Science, Xerox Corporation, and teachers, administrators, and schools throughout the country to engage in activities that they would otherwise have foregone. Without external support, AAAS would not have developed the program. Xerox would have seen fewer profits, or none at all, if it had to develop the program at its own expense. Teachers, administrators, and school systems would not have been inclined to seek out information about the program on their own or to mount training programs on the scale undertaken by AAAS and other federally subsidized efforts.

The federal government's significant involvement with direct subsidy to instructional materials research and development dates from two events in 1954, when Congress passed the Cooperative Research Act and the National Science Foundation initiated its Course Content Improvement Program. The Cooperative Research Act authorized the United States Office of Education to support educational research and development generally. NSF's Course Content Improvement Program sought to improve the methods and content of science curricula.

Later, spurred by the Soviet Union's launching of Sputnik I, Congress passed the National Defense Education Act (NDEA), which supported instructional materials research and development, among other objectives. At the same time, NSF intensified its own research and development programs. The National Defense Education Act was followed by the Elementary and Secondary Education Act (ESEA) of 1965, which authorized a nationwide chain of research and development centers, regional educational laboratories, and supplementary instructional centers to facilitate classroom use of research and development products. In 1972, the National Institute of Education (NIE) was created as part of an effort to rationalize federal subsidy programs in educational research.[1]

Some of the subsidies to research and development have been indirect. NDEA Title III and ESEA Title II authorized federal funds to support state and local purchases of instructional materials. By increasing the industry's sales and expanding its scale, these subsidies may have enhanced the capacity of firms to invest in research and development. Through its support of teacher training, the Education Profession Development Act may increase teacher receptivity to innovative technology and enhance rates of diffusion. NSF and NIE have supported basic research into learning processes, expanding the scientific knowledge available to developers of instructional materials.

Some indirect subsidies come from programs and institutions not directly concerned with public education or instructional materials. Techniques developed to improve military training have many civilian applications. Project TACT, supported by the Advanced Research Projects Agency (ARPA) in the Department of Defense, has investigated some of the problems lying at the threshold of computer-assisted instruction. ARPA has also indirectly contributed to instructional materials research and development through its massive subvention of research in artificial intelligence generally. Efforts supported by the National Institute of Mental Health to train emotionally disturbed children may also have research payoffs for the instructional materials industry.

Not all subsidies come from Washington or from government. In a very real sense, local school districts subsidize instructional materials development when teachers prepare materials for use in their own classes. A Rand study revealed the range of these local efforts. "Development activities," the study found, "ranged from a careful assessment of existing products or technologies, which were then repackaged into a form which reflected local interests and needs, to activities which, beginning from scratch, produced a wide range of project materials."[2]

Private foundations also play a role in supporting instructional materials research and development for the elementary grades. The Ford Foundation has been a leader in funding both basic and applied research. Since 1955 the foundation has helped to support Jean Piaget's work at the University of Geneva's Center for Genetic Epistemology. At the applied end of the research and development spectrum, Ford granted $180,000 to the University of Washington's Institute of Child Development for the development of learning programs for gifted children from poor or minority families.[3]

Other foundations have also been active, primarily in funding development activities. The Robert Wood Johnson Foundation made grants totalling more than $775,000 to the Lawrence Hall of Science between 1974 and 1976 to develop teaching materials for health education in elementary schools. In 1970 the George Gund Foundation gave $50,000 to the Educational Research Council of America to help in the production of social science curriculum materials for grades 4-6; the materials were later published by Allyn & Bacon in a social science series. Private foundations also support the work of institutions exclusively concerned with some specific aspect of instructional materials dissemination or evaluation. One example is a $5,000 award from the Mary Reynolds

Babcock Foundation to the Educational Products Information Exchange Institute to support EPIE's efforts to evaluate instructional materials.

Private support of research and development for the elementary grades should not, however, be overestimated. Foundations have been more generous in supporting research and development affecting instruction at the high school and college levels—although, to be sure, some of the findings produced by this research may be applied to problems in the elementary grades. (Typical grants to higher education that might contain significant spillover benefits for the lower grades are a $37,000 Exxon Education Foundation grant to the University of Michigan for the development of computer-assisted instruction for remedial English classes, and a $273,000 Moody Foundation grant to Dallas Baptist College to develop curriculum materials for videotaped, individualized instruction.)

Also, the chief implement through which foundations have sought to enhance the education of elementary school children has been television programs, not instructional materials. Many of these awards have been aimed at the program development activities of the Children's Television Workshop (CTW). Apart from the many millions of dollars that the Ford Foundation has spent on educational television and public television generally, it has, together with the Carnegie Corporation, spent millions more for CTW's development of *Sesame Street* and *Electric Company*. Other foundations have also aided CTW. The Clark Foundation has spent $25,000 annually to bring CTW programs to day-care centers throughout Dallas. The John and Mary Markle Foundation, as part of its extensive support of CTW, awarded $7,000 to the Rand Corporation to conduct a feasibility study of new methods for evaluating *Sesame Street* and the *Electric Company*.

Although private foundations and state and local governments have played some role in the support of instructional materials research and development, federal policy has been at the center of modern discussion on subsidies. Two issues predominate. One involves the educational directions that subsidized activities should pursue. The other involves the appropriate structures for subsidized research and development.

In theory, subsidies can turn research and development away from directions dictated by present patterns of supply and demand and toward objectives considered more socially useful. In fact, efforts to channel subsidies in new directions have to be reconciled with the reality that programs and products diverging too sharply from entrenched selection patterns will not be used. The effects of this resistance on federal subsidies are magnified by the fact that public schooling has traditionally been the preserve of state and local government. Congress and those responsible for administering federal subsidy programs have carefully tailored their efforts to avoid local complaints of undue federal interference in matters of local concern.

Questions have also been raised about which structures for subsidized research and development will most effectively overcome resistance to innovation. Increasingly, the decision has been to simulate the structures that have evolved in private markets. University researchers and specialized research and development centers have been funded to initiate instructional programs. Regional educational laboratories and supplementary centers have been created, with a focus on product development. Publishers have been offered incentives to refine and disseminate developed programs, to gather information about their products' use, and to incorporate this information in the ongoing research and development process. As with efforts to redirect research and development, the most serious obstacles have lain in attempting to alter the structure of materials selection decisions.

Directions for Change

At one time the National Science Foundation inserted a clause in individual grants and curriculum development projects expressly recognizing "that traditional American policy places responsibility for the selection of subject matter used in the schools in the hands of appropriate school authorities." In the clause, the foundation stated its desire that the granted funds "be restricted in their use to the development of new instructional programs and materials and to the dissemination of information about them."[4] The clause aptly characterizes the prevailing federal sensitivity to traditions of state and local control over public schooling. Federal subsidy programs have historically tried to reconcile traditions of local rule with perceived needs for centralized efforts at instructional change.

National Science Foundation

Established by Congress in 1950, the National Science Foundation was charged to "develop and encourage the pursuit of a national policy for the promotion of basic research and education in the sciences."[5] Early efforts in this direction, mainly fellowships for graduate education in the sciences, were quickly found to be inadequate. Subsequent programs set their sights a step or two lower on the educational ladder. By 1956, the foundation was proposing training institutes in which college and high school teachers could "learn from first-rate researchers and expositors about the more important and unifying concepts in their field."[6]

The proposal typified NSF's approach to the problem of local prerogative. Generally, the approach was to increase the instructional alternatives available to schools and to create an awareness of these alternatives, but ostensibly to leave local decisions on curriculum content and instructional methods untouched. Invigorated training for high school and college science teachers seemed a good way to increase the quantity and quality of the nation's scientists without offending local interests. The program was elective. No new programs or personnel would be injected into the schools. Teachers who had already been entrusted by local communities with their children's schooling would simply bring heightened skills to the effort.

Yet, the safest route was not the most effective one. By the late 1950s it had become clear to the foundation that for change to take hold, training programs had to be supplemented by the more enduring forces of curriculum and instructional materials. The foundation's 1955 report announced the formation of a unit to fund proposals for curriculum development, and its 1958 budget made the first request for an allotment for a separate Curriculum Development Program. Changes in the program's name over the years reflect its gradual shift in focus from curriculum to materials. Initially called the Course Content Improvement Program, it became for a time the Curriculum and Instruction Development Program, and has more recently been labeled the Materials and Instructional Development Section.

By 1975, these programs had supported fifty-three curriculum projects, the first of which was the now famous Physical Science Study Committee, led by Professor Jerrold Zacharias of the Massachusetts Institute of Technology. Another, the Minnesota School Mathematics and Science Teaching Project (MINNEMAST), produced materials aimed at coordinating mathematics and science instruction in kindergarten and the primary grades. The project produced twenty-nine sequenced instructional units, and teacher and student manuals, printed aids, and kits of materials for each unit. The project also produced a resource handbook for teachers, *Living Things in Field and Classroom.*[7]

Projects under the Materials and Instruction Development Program are initiated and administered within formal guidelines adopted by the foundation. The first step in project development is a "needs identification and assessment." This step assumes that the need for a specific project can be identified through a literature search or other surveys, through a foundation-sponsored conference to assess needs, or through a formal call for proposals by the foundation. Proposals generated in any of these three ways are then reviewed by NSF staff and outside reviewers, including curriculum developers, scientists, and school teachers and administrators.

If the proposal is funded, the project director will assemble a staff, establish business procedures, and select trial centers to demonstrate the materials produced by the project. Once project topics are selected, writing teams produce materials, which are then tested in demonstration classrooms and subsequently revised if necessary. At some point in this process, the developer submits proposed procedures for announcing the availability of its materials for publication. If NSF approves these proposed procedures and if a publisher comes forward and is approved by the foundation, the developer and publisher enter into a contract for publication of the materials.

NSF apparently recognized that, having sponsored the research and development stages of these projects, it would be dangerous to become involved in marketing. Support at this stage might subject the Foundation to charges of intruding into local decisions and, possibly, to charges of unfair competition from publishers of materials developed without subsidy. A guiding principle in the development of course content projects was that "Foundation funds were not to be used to promote the adoption of any specific curriculum, course or instructional materials; they were expected to compete on their own merit. Thus, a project's commercial publisher, not the Foundation, will often support marketing and teacher training efforts."

The foundation has indirectly supported dissemination activities in other ways. Summer institutes to orient secondary-level teachers to the new curricula formed an early approach to encouraging adoption of sponsored materials. Similar training efforts for elementary school teachers were less successful. Because elementary school teachers, unlike secondary level teachers, only rarely specialize in science instruction, an effort was made to train key elementary teachers and science supervisors, in the hope that they would influence others within their schools to favor adoption. The hope was not fulfilled and the program was terminated in 1966.

The foundation's more recent implementation programs have taken three forms: leadership specialist projects, teacher projects, and school system projects. Leadership projects may involve "information conferences" to acquaint school administrators with new curricula. Teacher projects are intended to prepare participating teachers to use the new materials effectively.[8] Because elementary teachers generally do not specialize, "proposals for elementary teacher projects must have the promise of large impact potential due to built-in multiplier factors for provision of instruction to a large number of teachers at low cost such as through the application of instructional technology." School system projects are aimed at introducing change to school systems that have already committed themselves to the innovation but need assistance in implementing it.

The recent controversy surrounding *Man: A Course of Study* (*MACOS*) highlights the hazards that attend federally directed efforts at curricular reform. Initiated by an NSF grant in 1963, *MACOS* is a social science program exploring the nature and sources of human behavior and is intended for use in the fifth and sixth grades. By 1974, the program had received $7 million in development and implementation funds and was being used in 1700 schools in forty-seven states. By 1975, the program was under attack from several quarters. Sales, according to one report, had declined by 70 percent.

The program was attacked for advancing immoral, irreligious views and for interfering with local autonomy. One Congressman called the program an "insidious attempt to impose particular school courses ... on local school districts, using the power and financial resources of the Federal Government to set up a network of educator lobbyists to control education throughout America."[9]

Apparently unconvinced by the foundation's efforts to restrict its activities to product development and dissemination, one official review group, appointed in the wake of the *MACOS* controversy, proposed to the House Committee on Science and Technology that "representative parents" be added to curriculum review and evaluation groups, and that the foundation avoid "undue influence, direct or indirect, over local decisions on curriculum adoption."[10]

The history of NSF programs suggests that this last injunction was unnecessary. The foundation has adopted a variety of procedures designed to avoid charges of interference with local adoption processes. In offering a wide range of programs, the foundation can say that it is only broadening the array from which state and local purchasing boards already choose. In training teachers and administrators, it can say that it is only sharpening the skills with which these choices are made. The complex structure of state and local decision making is not disturbed, and new possibilities are introduced for those who desire change.

The questions remain: how great the possibilities? How great the change? NSF's expedient policy of keeping its hands off local decision making implies that the level of innovation will not be high. Knowing that they cannot alter the generally conservative attitudes of local decision makers, the foundation and its grantees can be expected to shape their products to appeal to prevailing attitudes. Teacher training programs hold some promise of increasing the receptivity to change of these important decision makers. However, the teachers who elect to attend these programs are likely already well disposed to innovation, and training institutes apparently have little impact in the elementary grades.

NDEA III and ESEA II

Cash grants to state and local authorities to purchase instructional materials are even less intrusive than curriculum programs like those financed by NSF. Federal objectives are served through the conditions imposed on the grant. State and local interests are respected through the generality with which the conditions are stated. Even if the conditions are stated narrowly, the recipient enjoys considerably more freedom of choice than when presented with a federally financed curriculum program on a take-it-or-leave-it basis. The 1958 National Defense Education Act and, to a lesser extent, the 1965 Elementary and Secondary Education Act each employed this approach in authorizing grants for instructional materials purchase.

NDEA Title III provided for grants to state and local education agencies to support their acquisition of instructional equipment and materials other than textbooks. Title III's initial concern, that contemporary instruction in science, math, and foreign languages was inadequate to modern technological and strategic demands, was eventually broadened in response to pressures to give recipients greater freedom in selection. Since 1958, Title III has been amended to make all academic subjects eligible for funding. Another change authorized grants to local educational agencies "for the acquisition of equipment and materials . . . to be used in programs and projects designed to meet the special educational needs of educationally deprived children in school attendance areas having a high concentration of children from low-income families. . . ."[11]

A breakdown of Title III expenditures in fiscal year 1962 indicates the program's relative emphases. In that year the federal government contributed $40.9 million, which was matched by $45.5 million in state and local funds. Of the total, over 98 percent was committed to the purchase of equipment and materials.[12] Equipment items included audiovisual equipment, such as television and film projectors, and laboratory equipment such as microscopes and biological models. Materials included films and film strips, records, tape recorders, maps, globes and charts.

ESEA Title II continued NDEA's basic approach to financing instructional materials purchases with some strings attached. Title II's main difference is its reflection of ESEA's specific concern with the relief of poverty. Where NDEA Title III specified the kinds and subject matter of materials to be purchased, ESEA Title II focused on the relative need of a state's children and teachers for library resources and textbooks generally. Title II established a program supporting "the acquisition of school library resources, textbooks, and other printed and published instructional material for the use of children and teachers in public and private elementary and secondary schools." Payment was conditioned upon approval of a state plan specifying the criteria to be employed in selecting materials and establishing a program for the plan's execution, including the "development and revision of standards relating to library resources, textbooks and other printed and published instructional materials. . . ."

H.R. 16572, H.R. 4916. Other approaches have been proposed for accommodating federal, state and local interests concerning innovation in instructional materials. One bill, H.R. 16572, structured the federal role around the distribution of product information to state and local agencies. Another, H.R. 4916, proposed carefully conditioned grants to local agencies for educational technology programs.[13] Although neither bill has been enacted, each suggests methods that may be followed in the future.

The approach taken in H.R. 16572, "to establish a Council on Educational Technology in the Department of Health, Education and Welfare," was to have a small, highly centralized institution dispense information to prospective users of instructional materials. The council, consisting of fifteen members, was to "assess the quantity and quality of use of various types of technology in educational settings, including educational consumer reactions and evaluations of this technology." It was also to "encourage and support the testing and assessment of technological equipment being marketed for educational purposes and the publication and dissemination of test results."

Under the second proposal, H.R. 4916, funds would be applied to sequenced grants to local educational agencies. In the first phase of the sequence, funds would be allotted to planning for the development and implementation of "educational technology programs, involving the use of appropriate technology and material." The plan, covering a period of at least four years, would be required to describe present and projected educational needs of children in the area served by "the local educational agency, and propose a schedule for meeting and solving these needs and problems through the implementation of a comprehensive program of educational technology in sufficient magnitude to make a substantial impact on these needs and problems. . . ."

In the second phase, once planning had been completed, a local educational agency would receive funds to conduct training programs to strengthen the capabilities of the staff in elementary and secondary schools "to use and apply technology in the educational process." After the training program had made "sufficient progress," the agency would receive funding to acquire or rent "technological equipment and materials."

Funds granted to the state would be administered under state plans specifying the timing and conditions for local educational agencies' participation. The plan would also provide for the state's adoption of procedures to evaluate "the effectiveness of the program and projects supported under the state plan," to disseminate the results of these evaluations, and to adopt "promising educational practices developed through such programs and projects."

In addition to alloting 10 percent of the appropriated funds in support of educational technology research in elementary, secondary and higher education, the bill proposed two mechanisms for buttressing state and local dissemination efforts. First it encouraged the development of courses for training prospective elementary and secondary school teachers in the uses of instructional technology. Presumably, this would enhance state and local receptivity to innovative products. Second, by conditioning state eligibility for funds upon a state's creation of an "advisory council on educational technology," the bill would have encouraged the development within each state of a centralized, expert body that could promote and coordinate activities to augment those contemplated by the bill.

Neither H.R. 16572 nor H.R. 4916 could be expected to break through existing patterns of local resistance to innovation in instructional materials. Yet each in its own way might have advanced innovation to some degree. H.R. 16572, which proposed a Council on Educational Technology, would have helped to reduce the information costs that might disable otherwise innovative teachers, schools, and school districts from learning about inventive materials. It also would have supplemented statutory learner verification programs and private nonprofit organizations in providing information about the efficacy of instructional materials.

H.R. 4916, which proposed local education technology programs, was far more adventurous in its efforts to avoid interfering with traditions of local control. By combining the substantive focus typical of NSF programs with the local autonomy allowed by grant programs like NDEA III and ESEA II, it would have attempted to resolve two major problems with a single stroke, essentially giving states and localities the money to develop innovative programs on their own. Though the concept is attractive, it would doubtless encounter problems from another quarter: a severely limited number of trained personnel to conduct these programs. As will be seen, personnel limitations were significantly responsible for the failures of far less ambitious federal programs aimed at altering the structures for change.

Structures for Change

Reflecting on NDEA Title III, the chairman of the House Select Subcommittee on Education observed, "We know all too well how easy it is for hundred dollar projectors, thousand dollar video recorders and ten thousand dollar language laboratories to end up unused, tucked away in some musty basement where they are ignored by teacher, student, and administrator alike."[14] Early federal subsidy programs like NDEA focused mainly on research and development and assumed that the innovated materials would find their own way into the classroom. When it became clear that schools were not adopting and using these materials, new programs were introduced which aimed not only at research and development but also at overcoming the last few hurdles, from production through distribution and use.

Among the painful lessons learned was that attempts to integrate research, development, dissemination, and use can be sustained only by lengthy and systematic efforts. Also, traditions of local control and teacher and school resistance to innovation are not the only obstacles. One obstacle is that the federal bureaucracy that supervises instructional materials programs has many of the same conservative tendencies as the state and local bureaucracies that are supposed to adopt the programs. Schools seek materials that will satisfy the widest possible constituency. Grantors, wanting their programs to succeed, aim their efforts in the same direction.

Another impediment is the abruptness with which federal subsidy programs are enacted and amended and the speed with which results are demanded. Haste not only produces ill-conceived programs, it also makes it difficult to mobilize the needed numbers of qualified research and development personnel. Graduate programs in educational research are a relatively recent phenomenon; as a consequence, personnel have been in short supply even under the best of conditions.

These obstacles and others recur in the history of federal subsidy programs for research and development in instructional materials, beginning with NDEA Title VII, followed by ESEA Titles III and IV, and then by the amendments creating the National Institute of Education. The progression marked by these statutes is not only from an isolated conception of research and development to an integrated process of research, development, dissemination, use, and testing.

It is also a progression from possibly dramatic research ideas to products that seek to do no more than meet the ingrained preferences of those who purchase instructional materials.

NDEA Title VII

The National Defense Education Act of 1958 represents Congress's first major, defined commitment to research in instructional materials. NDEA Title VII authorized support for research and development in instructional technology and for programs to disseminate existing innovative techniques to the elementary through university levels. In its ten-year life the Title VII program encountered all the problems that would later plague its successors.

The origins of NDEA are popularly traced to the Soviet Union's launching of Sputnik I and to Congress's faith in educational investment as a way to meet the challenge posed by "the forces of totalitarianism." Other contemporary factors also pressed toward the solution chosen. One was the baby boom and the prospect of sorely taxed school personnel and facilities. Another was the technological growth experienced over the war years and the belief that at least some defense technologies could be converted to aid in the education of children.

Part A of Title VII, entitled "Research and Experimentation," specified that the commissioner of education, in cooperation with an Advisory Committee on New Educational Media, should through grants and contracts "conduct, assist and foster research and experimentation in the development and evaluation of projects involving television, radio, motion pictures and related media of communication which may prove of value to State and local educational agencies in the operation of their public elementary or secondary schools, and to institutions of higher education. . . ." To be included among these projects were "the development of new and more effective techniques" for using and adapting existing audiovisual methods and "for training teachers to utilize such media with maximum effectiveness," and "presenting academic subject matter through such media." Two vehicles were provided for these efforts: grants-in-aid "to public or nonprofit private agencies, organizations and individuals," and contracts with "public or private agencies, organizations, groups and individuals."

Part B, entitled "Dissemination of Information on New Educational Media," sought to enhance dissemination to potential users from elementary through university levels by authorizing the publication of materials, such as catalogues and abstracts, that would encourage informed use of newly discovered techniques. Also, the commissioner was authorized to provide technical assistance and demonstrations at the request of state or local educational agencies, colleges, or universities.

Of the approximately $40.3 million spent under Title VII, roughly 48 percent went into research programs under Part A, and 52 percent into dissemination programs under Part B. Experimentation with combinations of media drew the largest portion of funds, $15.8 million. Research into uses of television and programmed instruction attracted $9.4 million and $4.8 million respectively. Equipment developments outside the educational industries, such as in 8mm film projectors, audio cassettes, and tape recorders, were largely ignored.[15]

Congress extended the term of Title VII in 1961, 1963, and 1964. One of the 1963 amendments introduced "printed and published materials" as authorized research and development projects along with television, radio, and motion pictures. The expansion had been proposed at the 1961 hearings by the President of the McGraw-Hill Book Company and at the 1963 hearings by the President of the American Textbook Publishers Institute. The amendment may reflect an appreciation that the potential for important contributions lay as much in traditional forms as in the newer forms of instructional hardware.[16] It may also indicate that Title VII's sponsors and administrators were increasingly disposed to support research projects with which school users would be more familiar and therefore more comfortable.

NDEA Title VII spoke of research and development in the most general terms, and it was left to the Title's administrators to work out their program's agenda. The evolving preference was toward applied rather than basic research. One review reveals that Title VII "projects were overwhelmingly concentrated on instructional systems and practices," and that a "relatively small proportion of the projects were dedicated to more basic research in the learning process."[17] Despite this emphasis on applied research, the Title VII program was by all reports unsuccessful in introducing innovative products into the nation's classrooms. The most extensive single review of Title VII projects concluded that they "made no direct contribution to the development of and less than might have been expected to the specific production of widely used curricular materials."

One reason, no doubt, was that little if any concerted effort was made to get research results into the hands of school children. An early criterion for funding proposed Title VII projects was that proposals dealing exclusively with the development of instructional materials would not be considered eligible for support. In one canvass, a majority of project directors expressed the belief that the results of their Title VII projects had not been transformed into classroom practice. One reason they gave was that the information was still experimental and not properly disseminated.

Other factors also played a part in Title VII's failure to change the nature of instructional materials being used in the nation's classrooms. One was the unsettled state of research supervision in the Office of Education. Administration of Title VII had been assigned to a handful of permanent employees in the office, supplemented by academics appointed for terms of eighteen months or less. Yet the office was repeatedly being reorganized; in retrospect staff members viewed this as "disruptive to program continuity" and as inhibiting "sound goal-setting behavior." Also debilitating was the absence of any substantial tradition of educational research to lend direction and purpose to the program's agenda. During the decade that Title VII was administered, educational research remained significantly removed from contemporary advances in social science theory and methodology. This meant both that no informed consensus could be reached on which projects to support and that, because few individuals were trained in education research, there was a dearth of researchers to carry out the program.[18]

NDEA Title VII was the federal government's first major venture into instructional materials research and development. It soon became clear that for efforts of this sort to succeed, prospective users had to be made more receptive to the materials produced. So, for example, the Act was amended in 1964 to encourage the creation of training institutes for teachers and media specialists.[19] Also, structures had to be developed to coordinate the stages from basic research through product development, dissemination, and use. Title VII helped to support planning for two such structures, the research and development centers and the regional laboratories that would form the cornerstone of Title IV of the Elementary and Secondary Education Act of 1965.[20] Yet other problems could not be corrected by legislation or by programs. The lack of an educational research tradition, or research personnel in the needed numbers, and of steady direction from the Office of Education, continued to impede the efforts that followed NDEA.

Research and Development Centers

The Cooperative Research Act of 1954 authorized the commissioner of education to enter into agreements with universities, colleges and state educational agencies "for the conduct of research, surveys and demonstrations in the field of education." The early 1960s saw the creation of nine university-affiliated research and development centers. As originally conceived, the centers were to "concentrate human and financial resources on a particular problem area in education over an extended period of time in an attempt to make significant contributions toward an understanding of, and an improvement of educational practice in the problem area." Under this general charge, the centers were to pursue the entire continuum of innovative activity—research, development and dissemination.[21]

While early center efforts concentrated on basic research, by the mid-1970s many if not most of the centers were performing development and demonstration activities as well. The Wisconsin Research and Development Center for Cognitive Learning has, for example, maintained close liaison with Wisconsin's Department of Public Instruction. It has entered into contracts with nine state departments of public instruction to disseminate its products and programs and has entered into agreements with a group of developmental schools for implementing innovations.[22]

The centers may have been prodded in the direction of applied research by the findings of a 1964 government review of the Cooperative Research Program. Noting that the program had "stimulated qualitative improvement and quantitative expansion in educational research," the government report also observed that "the results of the projects ... did not lead directly enough or quickly enough to observable change and desired improvement in educational practice."[23] Whatever its impact on research and development center programs, this report clearly set the stage for passage of the Elementary and Secondary Education Act of 1965.

Regional Laboratories

ESEA Title IV continued the funding for the research and development centers. It also authorized the creation of regional educational laboratories. A letter from President Lyndon Johnson to Health, Education and Welfare Secretary John Gardner summarized the laboratories' agenda: "to overcome the lag between discovery and use, and to convert the results of years of research into application in the classroom."[24] Unlike the research and development centers, the laboratories were not to be connected to universities. Rather, each was to be "an independent nonprofit organization with its own governing board and management ... capable of making decisions regarding specific program objectives, attracting the resources—personnel, funds and facilities—necessary to realize those objectives and directing the operations by which these objectives would be obtained."[25]

Passage of ESEA and authorization of the laboratory program signalled a new, greatly accelerated phase in federal policy for education research and development. ESEA was signed into law on 11 April 1965. Over the summer of 1965 representatives from universities, public schools and state departments of education met to consider the role that laboratories might play in their respective regions. Working within guidelines issued by the Office of Education, these groups were spurred by the office's 15 October 1965 deadline for receipt of proposals. Between October 1965 and February 1966, office staff hurriedly sought to put proposals in shape for funding—obtaining more complete data from proponent groups, informally negotiating the terms of grants, and, where expedient, suggesting the merger of geographically proximate groups.[26]

On 15 February 1966 the Office of Education announced that twelve groups had been selected to receive planning funds for seventy-five-day development periods. Within forty-five days each was to file an interim report with the office, specifying the major educational needs of its region and the laboratory's programs and structure. A final report was due thirty days later. Site visits and consultations were conducted during this period by teams composed of academics and Office of Education staff. A slightly more relaxed agenda was followed in the initial funding of another eight laboratories.

By September 1966, one and one-half years after ESEA's enactment, twenty laboratories were at work under operational or development contracts. One month later, faced with mounting criticism of the work being performed by the fledgling laboratories, the secretary of health, education and welfare appointed a twelve-member National Advisory Committee to review the laboratory program. During the two months planned for the Advisory Committee's review, no new or increased funding was to be authorized for laboratory efforts.

The Advisory Committee's statement, adopted 12 May 1967, was guardedly optimistic about prospects for the labs. The committee found that "the funds allocated to date are not sufficient for carrying out the active work of the Laboratories," and that "the contract periods have been too short and too unstable to permit optimum program planning and achievement." Earlier in 1967, with the committee's conclusions already known, the Office of Education announced new funding levels and contract periods for all laboratories. Funding for each laboratory ranged from $300,000 to $1,800,000. Contract periods ranged from nine to twenty-one months.

The haste with which the laboratory program was begun precluded any serious effort to formulate objectives or to coordinate the work of the laboratories and the research and development centers. Indeed, the Office of Education guidelines had described the laboratories' mandate in terms that were essentially indistinguishable from those governing the research and development centers: the laboratories were to perform basic as well as applied research.

The role of the laboratories was further complicated by the introduction of supplementary educational centers, authorized by ESEA Title III. The stated purpose of these centers was to "stimulate and assist in the provision of vitally needed educational services" and "in the development and establishment of exemplary elementary and secondary school educational programs to serve as models for regular school programs." Because the laboratories were aimed at correcting instructional deficiencies in the schools in their regions, their efforts naturally blended into those of the supplementary educational centers. The main thrust of these supplementary centers was toward curriculum change and instructional services, but instructional materials were also a concern. In fiscal year 1969, for example, out of a total of 1,540 projects funded at $151,470,000, $31 million was allotted to sixty-seven projects to assess the efficacy of selected instructional methods, including individualized and programmed instruction. An added $24 million was spent on 122 projects aimed at demonstrating "the effectiveness of new educational technology, facilities, equipment, and materials," including "the use of television for instruction, computer assisted instruction, teaching machines, and instructional laboratories of all types."[27]

Concessions to pork barrel politics and to traditions of state and local control over elementary education added to the confusion about the laboratories' mandate. In the early stages of planning, there was strong sentiment for a comparatively small number of laboratories, each concerned with nationally rather than regionally defined educational issues. However, early in the congressional hearings on ESEA, the Department of Health, Education and Welfare apparently decided to call the laboratories "regional," not "national," and to shift their focus and prospective relations to a larger number of discrete regions across the country. Yet the hopes for national laboratories persisted, along with the nagging question of how to define a region properly. As late as July 1965, Office of Education staff were drafting preliminary guidelines for national as well as regional laboratories.

The operation of the Regional Educational Laboratories has stabilized since this period of initial turmoil and indecision. By the late 1960s, the laboratories had variously taken on regional roles, and product development and dissemination emerged as their major functions. The efforts of the Eastern Regional Institute for Education (ERIE) to install *Science—A Process Approach* are not atypical. These activities involved arrangements with surrounding school districts, with the state education departments of New York and Pennsylvania, with a network of college science education teachers, and with the National Science Foundation. Over 1300 teachers were trained to use the curriculum at ERIE summer institutes and workshops. With NSF assistance, fifty teachers of science and science methods were trained to support science curriculum innovation and improvement.[28]

The Elementary Science Information Unit, produced by the Far West Laboratory for Educational Research and Development, is another example of a dissemination tool developed by a laboratory. The Far West Laboratory asked two questions: Do teachers and administrators have enough time to find, gather, and process information about available new processes and products? Do researchers and developers adequately disseminate information that is readable and understandable? Negative answers to both spurred development of the Elementary Science Information Unit, a handsomely packaged multimedia kit describing six contemporary elementary science programs, including *Science—A Process Approach* and MINNEMAST. Development of the unit entailed an initial effort at conceptualization, production of a prototype tested on nineteen "target audience subjects," revision and field testing in nineteen schools with 181 "target users," revision and broader field use, and eventually development and distribution of the final product. Costs for the effort were estimated at $222,000. In the first four months, approximately 300 sales were made at $75 each.[29]

The laboratories have defined their objectives and solidified their administrative structures. But this does not mean that the objectives include significant innovation or that the administrative structures are capable of carrying it forward. Institutional failings identified by the 1966 Advisory Committee have persisted. As observed by the committee's chairman, Professor Francis Chase of the University of Chicago, "weakness built into the structure, the staff and the choice of activities by many of the Laboratories threaten to reduce the prospect that their performance will differ significantly from existing educational institutions."[30] In the years since this observation was made, many laboratories succeeded in bridging the gap between instructional materials research and classroom use. But the price of success may well have been acceptance of the educational conditions that it was hoped they would change.

Development of the *Kindergarten Program* by the Southwest Regional Laboratory for Educational Research and Development provides a good example of this phenomenon. The laboratory had evolved extensive formal relations for experimentation with schools in its region. Prepublication testing of the *Kindergarten Program* was probably more extensive than is customary in the private sector. The materials were tried out on students in successive stages of development, and teachers, administrators, and parents were queried about the program's implementation. But, perhaps as a consequence of these many consultations, the program finally produced "contains no really startling element. The materials have a conventional format and do not call for drastic behavioral changes on the part of the teachers." In the words of one evaluation group, "It is difficult to identify a single philosophy or unique theory of learning behind the program's development." In short, the processes and objectives under which the *Kindergarten Program* was developed can hardly be distinguished from those implicitly followed by private publishers without subsidies.[31]

One reason that the laboratories and the centers apparently failed to develop major research concepts into instructional products lies in a shortage of skilled workers. Applied educational research was hardly an established academic discipline, and the sources of trained practitioners were not equal to the needs of the mid-1960s. Government was not the only prospective employer. Industry and private foundations were also competing for talent, and probably on more favorable terms. Francis Chase, reflecting on the work of his Advisory Committee, noted that personnel shortages might not permit the effective operation of more than five to ten laboratories, far less than the twenty initially authorized.[32]

Some laboratories have sought to overcome personnel problems by persuading their social scientists to take responsibility for the full continuum of research and development activity—not only the formation of initial concepts, but also their development, field testing, and implementation. There are obvious disadvantages to this approach. Social scientists may not be particularly qualified to engage in dissemination, for their background is no more a credential for marketing than is the marketer's background a credential for social science research. Nor is there any real incentive for scientists' sustained involvement in dissemination. Professional recognition for scientists traditionally comes from basic rather than applied research. So long as these traditions continue, social scientists will hold back from applied research.

The Office of Education

On signing ESEA into law, President Johnson announced the formation of a task force to reorganize the Office of Education along lines consistent with the demands imposed by the Act. The reorganization, which went into effect in the summer of 1965, was vast and unsettling. Two particularly close observers of the office counted the toll: "Of thirty-six traditional divisions of the Office of Education, only two escaped major changes in level or function. Of twenty-five old super-grade personnel, only eight were unchanged in status or responsibility. Over twenty new super-grade jobs were established—to be filled principally from the outside."[33]

Research and development programs were lodged in the only functionally oriented bureau created by the reorganization, the Bureau of Research. Each of the other three bureaus was oriented toward school level—the Bureau of Elementary and Secondary Education, the Bureau of Adult and Vocational Education, and the Bureau of Higher Education. This division into one functional and three grade-level bureaus was not uncontested. Some argued that a single research bureau could more effectively coordinate and implement the several federal research programs. Others argued that dispersing the research programs among the three grade-level bureaus could make them more responsive to the needs of practitioners at the respective grade levels. One result would be increased opportunities for adoption and use.

The internal structure adopted for the Bureau of Research reflected a concession to those who had argued the merits of dispersion. The Bureau was divided into grade levels: Division of Elementary–Secondary Research; Division of Adult and Vocational Research; and Division of Higher Education Research. Two other divisions were created for nongraded programs: The Division of Research Training and Dissemination and the Division of Laboratories and Research and Development. This last division became home for the centers and laboratories.

Without knowing more about the personnel that staffed the Bureau of Elementary and Secondary Education and the Bureau of Research, and about their respective relation with field users of instructional materials, it is hard to judge the merits of the decision to place the centers and laboratories in the charge of one rather than the other. It is also hard to judge the related decision to place responsibility for Title III's supplementary centers in the Bureau of Elementary and Secondary Education rather than the Bureau of Research. The decision appears to have reduced the chances for coordination between the laboratories and the supplementary centers, particularly in light of the strained ties between the two bureaus.[34]

The Bureau of Research was hobbled by the same scarcity of talent that afflicted the laboratories and centers. In ESEA's first year many positions went unfilled and there was considerable turnover among personnel, particularly in the Division of Laboratories and Research and Development. For almost two years the division was headed by a succession of acting chiefs.[35]

The National Institute of Education

A federally funded national institute to conduct and sponsor educational research and development had been proposed at least as far back as 1958, as part of the federal education initiative that was then emerging. Succeeding years saw the proposal repeated and modified in the scholarly literature and in reports of government panels and commissions. Indeed, the regional laboratory program itself evolved through a process of political compromise from initial proposals for a system of national education laboratories.

President Nixon's 1970 education message to Congress gave a definitive shape to the proposed National Institute of Education and laid the foundation for its creation. As envisioned by the Nixon message, the national institute would have "a permanent staff of outstanding scholars from such disciplines as psychology, biology and the social sciences, as well as education," and "would conduct a major portion of its research by contract with universities, nonprofit institutions and other organizations." Sensitive to state and local interests, the Nixon message focused on the proposed institute's capacity to evaluate innovations in classroom teaching rather than to influence local decisions on curriculum and instructional materials.[36]

Of the four exemplary areas Nixon identified as appropriate for the institute's exploration, one—"television and learning"—was specifically concerned with instructional materials. Characteristically, the message focused on the hardware, not the software, for instructional innovation. Setting as a goal the increased use of the "television media and other technological advances to stimulate the desire to learn and to help teach" the message asked, "How can new techniques of programmed learning be applied so as to make television sets an effective teaching aid? How can audiovisual aids, the telephone, and the availability of computer libraries be combined to form a learning unit in the home, revolutionizing 'homework' by turning a chore into an adventure in learning?"

The National Institute of Education was established by the Education Amendments of 1972, substantially as conceived in the President's message. The amendments provide for a National Council on Educational Research, authorized to "establish general policies for, and review the conduct of, the Institute," and for a director of the institute to execute these policies. The Act specified that at least 90 percent of the funds appropriated for any fiscal year be spent through grants or contracts with public or private agencies and individuals, thus restricting the institute's in-house research.

The institute has supported the research, development, and dissemination of instructional programs and materials. Among its projects have been experiments with "computer-based instruction for disadvantaged elementary school students," focusing on "the long-term effect of such instruction on children's cognitive and affective development." In fiscal 1974 the institute supported the dissemination of sponsored projects, such as individualized programs in reading and math, upon a showing of their educational efficacy, their significance in meeting a major educational problem and the overall adequacy of the dissemination plan. The institute has also requested funds "to develop sampling plans, design and test survey materials, and prepare for a large scale survey of teachers, principals, school board members," in an effort to assure that "research and development programs are more closely directed to the actual needs of the education practitioner."[37]

Not all of the institute's programs were new. When the Office of Education was reorganized, the institute's Task Force on Education Technology and Productivity took over several Office of Education programs in instructional technology. One was to sponsor "major new initiatives in research, planning and evaluation of technology activities."[38] Other programs were retained by the Office of Education in a new Office of Educational Technology. Under the reorganization, the Office of Educational Technology was to take charge of nondevelopmental activities such as monitoring ESEA Title III technology projects.

Among the more extensive research and development programs transferred to NIE were those involving seven early childhood education centers and research training and dissemination research activities. The institute also took over the operation of ERIC, a computer-based information retrieval system originally conceived in the Office of Education. ERIC was intended to expedite research and development by enhancing the flow of educational research information among researchers, instructional materials producers, and teachers. By the close of 1976, ERIC's data base consisted of more than 113,000 education-based documents, gathered, screened and abstracted by sixteen clearing houses nationwide. Through its *Current Index to Journals in Education*, ERIC offered access to an additional 137,000 articles.[39]

NIE also inherited responsibility for eight research and development centers and eleven regional laboratories. Coincidentally, at about the time that the institute was getting its programs under way, the budget mechanism for supporting laboratory and center activities was shifting. Each laboratory or center had annually negotiated a single support contract; under the new mechanism, federal support would be provided project by project. One effect was that new entrants began to compete for contracts with the laboratories and centers. By enabling NIE to choose from among the projects proposed by the laboratories, the centers, and their competitors, the new contracting method created the possibility for centralizing in a single institution decisions on the direction of educational research and development.

Yet institutional and political forces continue to pull in the opposite direction. The laboratories and centers antedate the institute by several years. They have established their own political constituencies and have always been in a position to influence if not dominate institute decision making. Organized as the Council on Education Development and Research (CEDaR), the laboratories and centers have lobbied vigorously in the House and Senate, seeking continued institutional recognition. They have had a part of the NIE budget earmarked for their use. A 1975 consultant's report to NIE and the National Council on Educational Research concluded that "the CEDaR group members have been the single most important continuing pressure on the policy at NIE."[40]

As originally conceived, the National Institute of Education was to compare in prestige, visibility, and centrality to the National Institutes of Health. Its function was to stimulate and systematize the nation's program for educational research and development, a program that, in terms of the task to be accomplished, was "too small, too diffuse, maldistributed, too narrow in scope and lacking in non-academic institutions."[41] Because the institute inherited all of the problems and many of the institutional structures that preceded it, its efforts have been severely hampered. In addition to shortages in trained personnel, indecisiveness about goals, and a reluctance to encroach on state and local preserves, the institute has encountered the political inconstancy that has disrupted most educational research subsidy programs. Congress has come nowhere near approaching the level of support implied by its initial authorization of $550 million over three years. From a spending level of $142.6 million in the institute's first year, the institute was granted $75.7 million in its second year and $70 million in the third year, against budget requests of $188 million and $134 million respectively. And Congress has increasingly tried to confine the institute's discretion by earmarking as well as reducing the agency's budget.[42]

Unchanging Structures

To some, the erratic progress of federal subsidy programs, from the Cooperative Research Act of 1954 to the 1972 Educational Amendments creating the National Institute of Education, may be cause for optimism. Each of these programs was enacted in response to a perceived technological or social need; perhaps whenever important needs press for political resolution, programs and funding will materialize. Yet the haste with which these programs are first embraced and then abandoned has real costs. As the experiences of the Office of

Education show, political inconstancy gives programs little chance to develop in clear directions and gives personnel scant incentive to acquire the specialized training needed to execute these programs effectively.

If Congress and the federal bureaucracy were to mobilize behind a focused and sustained research and development program, would it make a difference? The succession of programs from NDEA VII through NIE reflects an increasing awareness that widespread dissemination and use of innovative instructional materials will not be accomplished by subsidies aimed simply at research and development. Subsidies to introduce these programs into schools are also needed. Yet as the continuum of research, development, and dissemination unfolded, it became clear that effective dissemination would require either intruding on perceived local prerogatives or reducing initial research goals to terms acceptable to local schools. The experience of the regional educational laboratories suggests that the latter occurred.

Against all the structures created by federal research and development programs, one other structure has refused to yield: the structure of public schooling in America through which state agencies, local boards, and classroom teachers decide what materials will reach the hands of students. Without dramatic changes in the schooling environment, federal subsidy programs for research and development in instructional materials cannot be expected to yield dramatic results.

6 New Paths for Research, Development, and Dissemination

To a lawmaker in the early 1960s, the remedy for the nation's newly perceived educational deficiencies must have seemed simple. More spending on instructional innovation could make education more effective and efficient. Yet it soon became clear that money alone was not the answer. Even the most generously funded research and development programs for instructional materials failed to fulfill the hopes of their sponsors. Bureaucratic resistance and entrepreneurial indifference were the real sources of this failure, and the means for successfully reversing them consistently eluded federal policy makers.

Then and now, the principal force working against instructional innovation is the decision-making structure of American schools. Materials selection is an accommodating process, open to pressures from federal, state, and local education administrators, school boards, principals, teachers, parents, students, and voters. In seeking to reconcile these forces, schools quite naturally select the texts and other materials that are least likely to offend any. As a practical matter this means materials that are very much like those already in use, with just enough surface differences to give the impression of change and to make the selection process appear worthwhile. The entire thrust of the selection process is to preserve the status quo.

This pattern of resistance is reinforced by the fact that schools rely almost entirely on private firms for their materials. Patterns of consumer demand necessarily determine the direction of private investment in research and development. Firms see little profit in innovative materials that their school customers will not mobilize to adopt. They direct their efforts instead to well-worn paths, adding just enough surface touches to suggest freshness. Furthermore, although firms occupy an important place in the research and development continuum, they have virtually none of the tools needed to carry out an innovative role. School resistance aside, firms do not incorporate dramatically inventive ideas in their products because the educational research establishment has not made enough of these ideas available in useful form. Also, none of the intellectual property systems—copyright, patent or trade secrets—offers strong incentive to investment in instructional materials research and development.

On its face, there was nothing wrong with the federal decision to spur educational advances by spending money. In theory, subsidies can overcome both consumer resistance and producer indifference. Consumer resistance can be overcome through teacher training and wide-scale dissemination of materials at no direct cost to the schools involved. Producer indifference can be overcome with more overt monetary incentives—direct grants for the production of innovative materials. Yet federal subsidy programs for instructional materials have proved hardly more innovative than the trends they were intended to reverse. One reason is the shortage of qualified personnel to carry on the subsidized research. Another, more enduring cause is the political environment in which funding decisions are made, an environment in which initially innovative federal efforts are constantly modified to avoid upsetting more conservative state and local traditions. Politics also means that funding will be mercurial. The flow of federal funds for state and local purchase of instructional materials and for support of research and development has been turned off by the Congress or impounded by the Executive as abruptly as it has been turned on. This uncertainty is hardly conducive to the sort of long-term planning and investment by schools and firms that is necessary for significant innovation.

If the programs of the early 1960s contain any single lesson, it is that the factors affecting innovation in instructional materials are numerous and intertwined, and that it would be hazardous to rest policy recommendations on even the best analyses of any one or two factors. Tyll van Geel concludes his meticulous survey, *Authority to Control the School Program*, with the observation that "today control of the school curriculum is shared by all three levels of government, by the state and federal courts, by the teachers' union, and in a minor way, by parents."[1] Yet it would be a mistake to assume that the consequent centralization of school decisions offers an enhanced environment for change in instructional materials or that the concurrence of the controlling forces would in itself guarantee innovation. Producer indifference aside, the institution of the neighborhood school and persistent traditions of uniform schooling assure that instructional materials will continue to reflect the lowest common denominator of community wishes.

The most effective solutions will be those that account for all of the main forces affecting the instructional materials marketplace and that come closest to satisfying affected constituencies without sacrificing change. The regional laboratories and research and development centers are the closest approach so far to such a solution, but offer far from a complete answer. Pursuing acceptance by schools and teachers, these institutions, particularly the centers, have been criticized for forsaking their basic research and development mission. Yet, the history of the labs and centers, and of federal subsidy efforts generally, suggests that these institutions may very well be as far as the nation can realistically hope to go in changing school materials without entirely changing the structure of schooling.

Larger changes can be expected only from dramatic alterations in the institutions that shape the level and direction of investment in instructional materials research and development. Without substantial changes in the structure of incentive systems, private firms cannot be expected to increase the level of their investment in research and development. Without substantial restructuring, the American school system will never channel research and development into more specific and effective directions.

Changing the Level of Change

Investment in instructional materials research and development could be increased in several ways. Prizes might be offered to the first firm that comes up with instructional products which meet specified performance criteria. A recent bill before the United States Senate did this for specific inventions by authorizing a National Science and Technology Awards Council to publish annually a list of no more than ten "most wanted scientific breakthroughs," and to award prizes ranging from $5,000 to $150,000 to the first person to meet the performance criteria established by the council for each category.[2] Government could also use tax incentives to stimulate investment in materials development. One approach would be to allow publishers and audiovisual producers to deduct editorial, development, and improvement costs as current expenses rather than as expenditures that must be capitalized and then amortized over the life of the copyright for the work produced.[3]

Whatever the appeal of these and other alternatives, intellectual property systems and direct subsidy programs will probably continue to occupy the mainstream of efforts to alter investment behavior. Undoubtedly, both these forms of government intervention could be revised to increase investment more effectively. One threshold problem for intellectual property reform is that materials research and development is too narrow an endeavor to justify sweeping revisions in the much more broadly gauged intellectual property laws. It would for this reason be more realistic to propose revision aimed at larger concerns, such as copyright or patent protection for computer software, that will incidentally cover important elements of instructional materials, such as software for instructional programs. A second task for reform is to restructure federal subsidy programs to give private publishers greater incentive to develop and disseminate ideas generated by federally supported research.

Intellectual Properties

Copyright and patent law today offer no incentive to investment in significant research and development of instructional materials. Because copyright protects expressions but not ideas, it provides no incentive to invest in the discovery or development of ideas. Patent law protects ideas but does not protect formats like those in which instructional techniques will characteristically be embodied.

The future of private incentive for instructional materials research and development is probably tied to prospects for broadened protection of computer programs under the copyright or patent laws, or under some entirely new intellectual property system. The affinity between computer programs and instructional programs goes beyond the obvious overlap represented by programs of computer-assisted instruction. Computer programs and instructional programs share a common central aim: the efficient achievement of distinct objectives through a series of discrete, interrelated, and specified steps. A legal system designed to protect the procedures and methods of computer programs could also offer substantial protection to instructional programs.

The critical question is whether future systems for protecting computer programs will offer incentives to bold innovation or will be hobbled by the doctrines and attitudes of the present intellectual property systems. Copyright protection for computer programs has in theory been available since 1964, when the Copyright Office first announced that computer programs were acceptable for registration.[4] On its face, the 1976 Copyright Revision Act, protecting "original works of authorship fixed in any tangible medium of expression,"[5] does not disturb the position that computer programs are copyrightable. The real limitation on copyright protection for computer programs and instructional programs lies in the Act's provision that "in no case does copyright protection for an original work of authorship extend to any idea, procedure, process, system, method of operation, concept, principle, or discovery, regardless of the form in which it is described, explained, illustrated, or embodied in such work."[6] It remains to be seen, however, whether the new Act will be interpreted or amended to extend definitive protection to computer programs, and whether courts will take this expansion as a cue to allow copyright protection for a program's method as well as its expression.

The extent of patent protection for computer programs is also in doubt. The Patent and Trademark Office and the Court of Customs and Patent Appeals have at different times given different answers to the question whether computer programs are patentable.[7] The Supreme Court has twice had the opportunity to answer the question, but it sidestepped the issue both times.[8] The 1966 report of the President's Commission on the Patent System proposed that computer programs be excluded under any new patent legislation, and this proposal has been carried forward in revision bills pending before the Congress.[9] Patent protection for instructional programs is even more questionable than protection of computer programs generally, in light of the patent law's historic aversion to subject matter that incorporates elements of human behavior.

Future protection for computer programs and instructional programs may very well come not from copyright or patent but from congressional enactment of a program protection law specially shaped for research and development in this sort of subject matter. The outlines of one widely discussed proposal suggest how intellectual property can be shaped to protect investment in instructional materials research and development.[10] Under this proposal, statutory subject matter would be divided into: (1) the general concept underlying the program to be registered; (2) the program itself, in the form of a sequence of instruction; and (3) a detailed description of the program. The last two elements, program and description, would be protected by the proposed statute. Copies of both would be deposited with a designated registrar and kept secret by him or her for the statutory period.[11]

As under the copyright law, there would be no administrative examination of subject matter at the time registration is sought, other than for compliance with formal requirements. The system would protect only registrations of "relatively complex sequences," and would outlaw as infringement "any unauthorized duplication of a registered program, of a registered detailed description, or of a translation." At the time of registration, the originator would be required to "deposit with the registrar a copy of a document which describes the concepts utilized by the program." Failure to describe properly would render registration of the derived program unenforceable. Unlike the patent system, however, disclosure of the underlying concept would not result in its protection but rather in its forfeiture: "The registrar will publish and distribute copies of this conceptual description. . . . There is no liability if someone uses this published description of concepts to write a program which does the same thing as the registered program." The provision does, though, contemplate the concurrent availability of patent protection for the concept.

By excluding protection for basic concepts, this proposal would, like copyright and patent, offer virtually no incentive to investment in substantial basic research. The exclusion of protection for basic concepts should not be surprising, for it is connected to Congress's general reluctance to award private monopolies over fundamental ideas and discoveries, an attitude that is deeply rooted and likely to endure. This means that direct subsidies will continue to be the main source of investment in basic research and that unfettered access to basic research findings will continue to be the norm. It also means that the central challenge to policy making in the area will be to devise research and development systems that will produce needed new ideas under direct subsidy, that will allow open access to these ideas, and that will offer sufficient incentives to private producers to put these ideas into forms that can be marketed to schools and used by schoolchildren.

From Science to Technology

The problem of getting basic research findings implemented and disseminated is neither new nor unique to instructional materials research and development. One solution, widely employed in federal research programs, has been to grant private contractors limited copyright and patent rights for any products they may derive from the basic research. The solution raises a more specific but equally troublesome issue: to what extent and on what terms should property rights be transferred from the government which subsidized the research to the private firm which will implement it?

Many would argue that no rights should be transferred on any terms; if research has been publicly financed its results belong to the public without charge. According to this argument, it is unfair and inefficient to give monopoly rewards to a private entrepreneur who has paid nothing for the basic research and to penalize a public which must pay for it twice—first in the tax revenues allocated to the research program, second in the form of increased prices paid for the goods produced. According to this view, huge public benefits in the form of lower prices can be reaped by withholding patent and copyright protection from the results of federally financed research. The dramatic advances in American agriculture produced by government-funded research and dissemination programs are commonly cited as an example of the advantages of public subsidies unfettered by patents or copyrights.[12]

One answer to this argument is that, whatever their sources, *some* expenditures will always be needed to bring research findings into actual practice. Agricultural innovations were initiated and spread through two successive subsidies—the first to the laboratories that made the basic findings, and the second to the schools and county agents that disseminated them. Under the circumstances, publicly financed dissemination may have been more efficient than private dissemination induced by the patent incentive and paid for directly by consumers. This does not mean, however, that publicly financed or conducted dissemination will always be preferable.

Because some added expenditure is always needed to put research into practice, the only real question is how the price should be paid—by taxpayers through additional government subsidies, or by consumers through the increased prices that patented and copyrighted products command in the marketplace. The advantage of patent and copyright over public subsidies as an incentive to dissemination is that, by posing a risk of loss and a chance of profit, they encourage efficient behavior. If patent and copyright were withheld, dissemination could be accomplished by paying the publisher a flat fee to refine, print and distribute instructional materials. With government reimbursement guaranteed and monopoly returns prohibited, the publisher would have little incentive to produce materials that would appeal to consumers, or to economize in printing operations, or to pursue marketing activities vigorously. Patent, copyright, or other intellectual property systems may also be fairer than subsidy. When a publisher is repaid through sales of a work, it is the school district, which most directly benefits from the work, that pays. When a publisher is federally subsidized, the bill is paid by taxpayers across the country who benefit less directly, if at all. The relative inequity of public subsidies is less apparent in the case of agriculture, where the fruits of subsidized research and development are shared by all.

Both politics and economics suggest that, in the case of instructional materials, copyright and patent are the preferable means for supporting development and dissemination. An industry already exists for the production and dissemination of instructional materials and, as a political matter, legislators will probably hesitate to supplant market forces through subsidy. Further, with the MACOS controversy fresh in their minds, legislators can be expected to shrink from the confrontation with state and local traditions that a direct federal role in dissemination might produce. No such political fears were stirred by the dissemination of agricultural research findings. Finally, effective dissemination of innovative instructional materials will require a far more substantial and sustained effort than did the dissemination of agricultural research findings. Farmers were ready, indeed anxious, to employ agricultural lessons offered, once their productivity was demonstrated. Schools have no comparable incentive to be productive. The efforts needed to overcome their resistance will politically be far too expensive for the federal government to undertake.

The problem for policy is that political forces press in different directions. Arguments against copyright or patent protection for the products of subsidized research—arguments, essentially, against the giveaway of public funds—possess considerable popular and political appeal. It is no surprise to find this political conflict reflected in the grant policies of all major educational funding agencies. Nor, given the relative immediacy of arguments against government interference in local schooling, is it surprising to find a general trend toward giving private contractors a greater stake in patents and copyrights stemming from federally supported research. The licensing practices of the National Science Foundation, the Office of Education, and the National Institute of Education, the three agencies primarily responsible for education research, are illustrative.

National Science Foundation

The basic objective of the National Science Foundation's dissemination policy is "to achieve maximum educational benefits for all potential users"; educational benefits are to "take precedence over all other considerations including possible generation of income." The NSF policy seeks to insulate the foundation from local purchase decisions by delegating publication and distribution arrangements to private enterprise. It limits interference with normal competitive conditions in the publishing industry by encouraging open competition for distribution rights to project materials, and by setting royalty rates at levels that will not distort the industry's price structure.[13]

Under the NSF policy, the project grantee stands at the center of negotiations for dissemination of materials produced in the project. Once the grantee and foundation agree on commercial publication, the first steps are for the grantee to develop and for the foundation to approve a plan for securing a publisher. The grantee typically notifies publishers that its materials are available for commercial publication. If publishers are interested, the grantee then holds a conference with them and solicits formal requests to publish the materials. These submissions, which set out the publisher's proposed dissemination plan and royalty structure, are evaluated by the grantee, which then submits its selection for approval by the foundation. After foundation approval, the grantee negotiates a contract with the publisher, subject to final review by the foundation.

Copyright and royalty terms in NSF publication contracts have varied from year to year and from project to project. One early strategy, employed in the foundation's CHEM Study project, was to hire publishers only to print the materials, giving the grantee responsibility for distribution. Another early approach was to publish project materials in soft cover on a nonprofit basis, encouraging large-scale, nonexclusive copying of these materials by others, who then prepared commercial, hard-cover versions. Later policies involved variations on the grant of exclusive rights. One required grantee and publisher to provide for royalty-free use of the materials by other publishers after a specified period. Under a more recent policy, the period of exclusivity is based on the nature of the materials; regularly revised materials are ordinarily given a period of exclusivity that coincides with the expected revision period, typically four to six years.

Royalty rates vary. Among the factors that affect the negotiated rate are publication and distribution costs, the extent of the publisher's contributions, and the price of competing, privately developed materials. Originally, the publisher's obligation to pay royalties was limited to the period of exclusive right to publish the materials. In 1969 the foundation changed this policy to require continued royalty payments unless the publisher can demonstrate that it has not recovered its investment within the exclusivity period.

The foundation's patent policy, which has not been an issue in instructional materials dissemination, substantially follows the philosophy of its copyright policy. Hence the foundation's major objective is "to encourage the use of inventions arising out of activities supported by the Foundation. It is important that any useful product or process developed or improved under an award is made available to the public on reasonable terms."[14] In the case of institutional patent agreements, and in certain cases where principal rights in an invention are left with a grantee which itself is not expected to develop the invention further, the foundation establishes a general preference for nonexclusive licensing, but allows an exclusive license if the grantee finds it necessary as an incentive for the invention's development and implementation.[15]

Office of Education and National Institute of Education

At one time the Office of Education required that copyright be withheld from all the products it sponsored.[16] The office has since retreated from that position and now recognizes that exclusive but tightly limited terms of copyright may be needed to promote "the effective dissemination and use of USOE supported materials in a fair and equitable manner to all interested parties—developers, producers, and users."[17]

With some variation in emphasis and detail, the copyright policy followed by the Office of Education, and more recently the National Institute of Education, closely parallels the NSF policy. The grantee mediates between prospective publishers and the agency, negotiating contracts with publishers and seeking their approval by the agency. NIE and OE regulations call for somewhat more detailed documentation of the publication proposal than does the NSF policy. In requesting copyright authorization, the developer must include: the reasons that the materials should be disseminated under copyright; justification for the proposed copyright period; a list of prospective producers to be solicited; the estimated size and nature of the market for the materials; and criteria for selecting the publisher, including proposed publication timetable, price to be charged, and royalties to be paid.

The NIE-OE policy is particularly sensitive to the difficulties of alerting publishers to available project materials, and of obtaining competing bids on works that are not commercially attractive. The Publishers Alert Service, operated by NIE, regularly apprises about three hundred publishers and audiovisual materials producers of the availability for publication of materials prepared with funding from OE or NIE. Though the policy generally favors competition among publishing proposals, it reduces the grantee's obligation to seek out publishers for "thin market" materials—products "for which a limited market and consequently unsubstantial publication revenues are anticipated."

On its face the OE-NIE policy is less flexible about copyright and royalty terms than is the NSF policy. As a rule, the allowable copyright term may not exceed five years. In practice this limit is waived if the publisher can show that it cannot recoup its investment in that time, or if extending the term is the only way that a publisher can be attracted to the project. As to royalties, nonprofit grantees are permitted to choose either 50 percent of the net royalties or a percentage corresponding to the grantee's financial contribution to the project. Commercial contractors may retain royalties only to the extent needed to defray administrative expenses incurred in obtaining the publication of the material.

Toward More Effective Investment Structures

Invention in instructional materials requires basic research into learning behavior, the development of new learning strategies, and the incorporation of these newly apprehended principles and strategies into workable instructional products. The early stages of this process pose few conceptual problems for policy. Longstanding traditions of open access to basic research make closed, private incentive systems an unrealistic alternative to direct subsidy. Thus the range of realistic alternatives at this end of the research and development spectrum consists of more, fewer, or better directed subsidies.

The more challenging policy decisions lie in the implementation of research and development. Three alternatives, each with roots in current practice, offer some indication of the range of practical possibilities. One alternative is to increase the subsidies aimed at stimulating the development of basic research findings into usable instructional products and at enhancing the dissemination of these products. A second is to offer more generous intellectual property protection for the fruits of development activities. A third alternative is to organize development and dissemination activities around private firms with school consumers.

The first approach, direct subsidy to dissemination, deserves the least consideration, if only because it is the least likely to be adopted. Respect for local prerogatives has historically kept the federal education establishment away from direct involvement in implementation and dissemination. The MACOS controversy left no doubt of the strength of local resistance to direct federal intrusions or its ability to reverberate in the halls of Congress. Congressmen have little to gain by promoting a federal role in disseminating innovative materials, and congressionally funded agencies like NSF, NIE, and OE have much to lose by pursuing such a role on their own.

Alternatively, intellectual property policies could be reshaped to encourage greater private investment in the development and dissemination of basic research findings. One way would be to strengthen the forms of intellectual property protection available for instructional materials. Another is to make exclusivity the rule rather than the exception in awarding property rights to materials produced from subsidized research programs. These two steps would leave development and dissemination in the hands of private producers and thus avoid any appearance of federal involvement in local schooling. By making private investment in development and dissemination more rewarding, they might also encourage competition and new economies in production and marketing.

The third approach, typified by regional educational laboratories and research and development centers, may point the way to a politically acceptable path between objections to federal interference in local affairs and charges of giveaway to private industry. The laboratories and, to a lesser extent, the centers have become actively involved in marketing their products, particularly those with little appeal for commercial publishers. They can also enter into contracts with private firms to develop, produce, or market new types of instructional materials. Because the centers and labs are structurally independent of federal control, they enjoy some immunity from charges of improper interference in local affairs. Because they are nonprofit, they are also immune from charges of giveaway. Yet, despite their bright prospects, laboratories and centers also share a troubled history. Their success and the success of institutions like them will necessarily turn on their ability to be sufficiently independent from federal grantors to be insulated from the effects of mercurial funding patterns and to avoid charges of federal intrusion into local school affairs.

The problem of getting basic research findings implemented and disseminated in useful form is not unique to the instructional materials research marketplace; the prevailing patterns of consumer resistance to innovation are. More effective mechanisms for increasing the level of investment in instructional materials research and development are necessary, but not sufficient in themselves to make investment patterns more effective. The patterns of demand must also be altered.

Changing the Direction of Change

If any one fact about the prevailing direction of instructional materials research and development is clear, it is that investment is generally being channelled toward a uniform level of consumer interest. The main reason for uniformity is the institution of the neighborhood school and its implicit accommodation of contending interests. Uniformity in preference should not be mistaken for a national consensus on the goals of elementary schooling. Parents, teachers, administrators, and scholars differ sharply about schooling's proper objectives. Nor is the split simply between professionals and the public. Questions of value are at stake, and professionals themselves are deeply divided.

The present pattern of preference is not only uniform; it is also closely tied to the status quo. One reason for this attachment to the status quo is bureaucratic and political aversion to change. Another reason is that schools have no incentive to become more productive or to seek out materials that will help them teach more effectively.

It would be a mistake to recommend policies that directed instructional materials research and development along more diversified, individualized lines, for the resulting narrowly focused products would not be adopted or used in the neighborhood school. Substantial efforts to make instructional materials more effective would also probably be wasted. The largely unsuccessful efforts to mandate learner verification for instructional materials illustrate the futility of trying to change schoolbooks without changing the schools. Any hope for the success of innovative programs is closely tied to the success of more general proposals for school reform, such as accountability, performance contracting, and voucher systems. Each of these proposals includes the sort of structural changes needed to make the school environment more hospitable to change in instructional materials.

Accountability requirements, which hold teachers to specified standards of performance, may encourage teachers and administrators to select—and publish— the materials that will best help them to meet these standards. Performance contracts, which link payment and profits to the contracting firm's attainment of specified learning goals, will give the firm a real incentive to acquire effective materials. Accountability and performance contracting may stimulate the production of more effective materials, but cannot be counted on for more diverse materials, because neither system implies any change in the monolithic structure of school decision making. By contrast, voucher systems can produce diversity as well as efficacy. By simulating the marketplace and promoting differentiation among schools, voucher programs can generate diverse streams of demand for instructional materials, encouraging publishers to produce materials for specific school populations.

Accountability

The term "accountability" encompasses a wide span of efforts to make schools answer for the relation between the costs of schooling and its benefits as measured by increased student achievement. Legislation for school accountability dates back at least to the early 1960s, with Pennsylvania's 1963 School District Reorganization Act; it spread quickly across the country later in the decade.[18] Accountability legislation takes a number of approaches. Some accountability statutes require the adoption of statewide educational goals, usually in very general terms. Michigan's statute is typical, directing the state department of education to "establish meaningful achievement goals in the basic skills for students, and identify those students with the greatest educational need in these skills."[19] In a few states, accountability programs require local school systems to develop their own goals, but give no real guidance on the forms these goals should take. In at least nine states, accountability legislation requires the adoption of student performance objectives. In Florida, for example, the commissioner of education must develop "a uniform, statewide program of assessment to determine . . . achievement of approved minimum performance standards."[20] Several states have adopted performance standards for teachers. California's much-debated Stull Act, for example, ties evaluation of teacher performance to student performance.[21]

Accountability through private lawsuits, though widely discussed, is still in its infancy. Discussion has centered on a 1972 lawsuit, *Peter W. v. San Francisco Unified School District*.[22] The plaintiff, Peter W., graduated from high school in 1972. The allegations in his complaint depict Peter as an average student in every respect: a first-grade intelligence test revealed an average I.Q.; his attendance record was average; his grades were average; and at no time did his teachers indicate a need for special or compensatory instruction. Yet according to the complaint, the recently graduated plaintiff was, in fact, functionally illiterate and could not even read a job application form. Peter claimed damages for wages lost from restricted educational opportunities and additional damages to reimburse the cost of private tutoring. The complaint was eventually dismissed and an appeal was unsuccessful.

Though ultimately unsuccessful, the complaint in *Peter W. v. San Francisco Unified School District* does indicate the outlines of common law and statutory claims that may some day prevail. One count, that the defendant school system negligently "failed to use reasonable care" in discharging its "duties to provide plaintiff with adequate instruction, guidance counseling and/or supervision," essentially claimed professional malpractice, the sort of charge that disappointed patients and clients sometimes make against their doctors and lawyers. Another count, misrepresentation, charged that the defendants had falsely and fraudulently represented to Peter's parents that he was performing at or near grade level and needed no special assistance. Peter also claimed that the defendant had breached several statutory duties. One duty stemmed from provisions in California's Education Code requiring school authorities to keep parents advised of their children's educational progress.[23] Others were rooted in code provisions that school districts design their courses of instruction to meet individual student needs[24] and that no student receive a high school diploma without meeting minimum standards of proficiency in basic academic skills.[25]

A key advantage of any system of accountability through private lawsuits is that by assessing damages against school districts, it could force schools to quantify the immediate costs of not providing an adequate education. Faced with an aggregate of prospective damage awards, schools might begin to think about investing at least this amount in improving the quality of education to a point at which lawsuits could be effectively countered and damages avoided. Yet it is far from certain that a system of accountability through private lawsuits will ever materialize or, if it does, that the incremental educational benefits to be derived will justify the substantial social costs of litigation.

What about the relationship between accountability and improved quality of instructional materials generally? Accountability statutes rarely deal with instructional materials as a separate topic, and when they do it is in the most general terms. Specific mention of instructional materials is hardly necessary, though—the impact of accountability decisions and statutes on instructional materials will be closely tied to their impact on instruction. For example, if accountability requirements cause teachers to focus their efforts on getting students to perform well on standardized tests, then the most attractive materials will be those that help the teacher prepare students for the test. Also, if innovative teaching techniques are foregone out of fear that they will not pass muster under traditionally anchored teaching appraisals, innovative instructional materials will be avoided for the same reason.

To those concerned with change in instructional materials, the problem with accountability is not that it has little impact on the quality of instructional materials, but that it has little impact on the quality of instruction generally.

Filled with details about educational objectives and the procedures that should be followed in formulating them, accountability statutes only rarely address the crucial question of the sanctions to be employed against teachers and school systems that fail to meet the specified performance standards. Accountability statutes that do address the question of sanctions usually do so in loose, unenforceable terms. Another drawback of accountability statutes is that, to the extent that they are effective, they are likely to restrict diversity. Accountability standards are adopted uniformly across a state or, at the narrowest, across a school district. Thus, if explicit statutory criteria are effective as educational objectives, they will also be effective in quashing elements of diversity that may have survived the consensus decisions of public schools. Greater promise for increasing efficacy without sacrificing diversity would appear to lie in performance contracting.

Performance Contracting

The typical performance contract between a private firm and a public school system calls for the firm to provide instructional services and materials, with compensation scaled to the educational results achieved. At the heart of performance contracting is the notion that if firms are paid according to what they produce, they will produce more, and more efficiently, than will public schools not affected by the profit motive. Because contracts can be shaped to meet the needs of particular schools, or even of specific groups within a school, they offer greater opportunities to diversify instructional activities.

An early, federally supported experiment in Texarkana illustrates the performance contracting concept.[26] Faced with a serious need to improve the reading and mathematics skills of potential dropouts, two Texarkana districts requested performance contract proposals from 113 educational technology firms. A bidders' conference was then held for forty interested firms. Dorsett Educational Systems, a manufacturer of teaching machines, was selected as the contractor. The company's contract objective was to produce at least one year's gain in reading and math in eighty hours of instruction for each student. The base fee was $80 per student, with increments to be awarded for greater improvement but with no payment if a student did not gain at least one year in reading or in math. Performance was to be measured by standard achievement tests.

Instructional materials played an important role in the Texarkana experiment as well as in later performance contract experiments across the country. In fulfilling its contract, Dorsett relied heavily on its own teaching machines to diagnose student needs for sequences of programmed instructional materials. A sample of six contractors in eighteen other projects reveals varying but substantial use of teaching machines and reorganized texts and workbooks. One reason for the prominence of instructional materials is that their producers have been among the most active bidders for performance contracts. Along with Dorsett, RCA, McGraw-Hill, Macmillan, and Behavioral Research Laboratories had shown initial interest in the Texarkana contract.

The activities of Behavioral Research Laboratories (BRL), a large educational business firm, suggest the special role that instructional materials can play in performance contracting. Well before it got involved in performance contracting, BRL had marketed the Sullivan Reading Program, a series of twenty workbooks and ninety-two supplemental readers, as well as a mathematics program. In 1970 BRL agreed to take charge of the entire curriculum of the Banneker School in Gary, Indiana, for three years. The contract contemplated use of the Sullivan learning programs in reading and math. Payments were to be based on student achievement in these two areas. According to a Rand study, the experimental Banneker program placed "a much greater emphasis on materials"[27] than do conventional schools. In Philadelphia, BRL entered into an unusual performance contract based on its instructional materials alone. Providing teacher training but otherwise not becoming involved in the school's operation, "BRL essentially sold materials ordinarily costing $20 per set for $40 per set if a child advanced one grade on an achievement test in a year's time; if the child achieved less than a year's growth the cost to Philadelphia would be zero."[28]

Vouchers

Proposed voucher programs take various forms. Generally, all rest on the assumption that government should support but not control elementary schooling. These proposals typically have parents picking their children's schools, paying the schools with vouchers given to them and later redeemed by their local school districts. To survive, a school must attract enough vouchers to meet its costs of operation.

Like performance contracting, vouchers use the profit motive, or at least the survival instinct, to increase educational efficiency. Unlike performance contracting or accountability, vouchers also predicate educational diversity. By replacing the public school monopoly with a regime of free competition, vouchers aim to produce a variety of schools serving interests that are sufficiently broad to assure full classrooms, but sufficiently narrow and specialized to attract parents with distinct educational concerns for their children. Vouchers can, in short, break down present patterns of uniformity, allowing schools to differentiate along the lines of interest expressed by the parents of their potential consumers.

Adoption of the voucher idea across the country would doubtless revolutionize the direction, and possibly the level, of investment in instructional materials research and development. Required for the first time to satisfy specific consumer interests, schools could be expected to make substantial performance demands on instructional materials. Producers would be given an incentive to invest in research and development of more efficient instructional tools with more precisely focused educational goals.

All of this is only speculation, for there is little evidence so far on the operations of the voucher schools. The first and most talked about voucher experiment, in the Alum Rock Union School District in San Jose, California, involved only public schools and departed from the typical voucher model by assuring participant schools of continued funding apart from market demand. In the words of one evaluator, these modifications "raise serious questions as to whether the Alum Rock demonstration is a voucher system at all."[29] Thus, little can be inferred from the ways in which Alum Rock schools used instructional materials. The fact that the schools spent, on the average, 60 percent of their discretionary funds on instructional materials, as compared with 16 percent, 9 percent, 8 percent, and 6 percent for aides, equipment, teachers, and field trips, respectively, is at best suggestive.[30]

At this point, the prospects for vouchers look slim. Well-entrenched constitutional and political traditions stand between the voucher idea and its realization. For a school district to give vouchers for public and private but not to parochial schools may be seen as discrimation against religion, in violation of the United States Constitution's free exercise clause. Yet aid to parochial schools may violate the constitutional prohibition against aiding in the establishment of religion.[31] Vouchers also raise Fourteenth Amendment problems because they could be intentionally used to reestablish segregated schools or because independent parental choice might lead to resegregation. State constitutional traditions of uniformity in education will also be hard to shake, as will the tradition of the neighborhood school.[32]

Conclusion: Paths for Change in Instructional Materials

Almost everything that is known about schools in America underscores their resistance to change. Accountability, performance contracting, and vouchers are only examples of the proposals that have been crushed or compromised in the network of federal, state, and local politics. Accountability has succeeded in clarifying school goals, but only in the most general, ineffectual terms. Despite some demonstrated successes, experiments with performance contracting were early cut short because of a sudden lack of interest within the federal education bureaucracy. Voucher programs have also foundered. Schools resist technical innovation with as much force as they resist structural and social innovations like accountability, performance contracting, and vouchers.

Patterns of resistance are closely intertwined, and social and structural innovations in the schools are necessary predicates to technical innovation. If schools do not change, there is little hope of instructional materials' becoming more effective or diverse. Preoccupied with maintaining the status quo, instructional materials selection agencies hardly offer an attractive environment for investment in research and development for new materials. And structural change, though a necessary condition to technical change, is not a sufficient one. Publishing firms and audiovisual materials producers, though given few incentives to support investment in research and development, continue nonetheless to be the main source of instructional materials in this country. Federal subsidy programs, which two decades ago offered the greatest hope for instructional change, have been consistently thwarted by traditions of deference to local autonomy and by lack of sustained funding and experienced personnel in the needed numbers.

With school systems so resistant to change, it is tempting to look outside the school, into homes, streets, and playgrounds, for signs of change in the instructional materials that children use. Here, unconstrained by school choice, parents and children are free to buy and use the books, programs, and games that they find most appealing. Television programs like *Sesame Street* and *Electric Company* are only the most conspicuous examples of the nonschool avenues through which children are educated today. Educational publishers already distribute their products through outside channels—bookstores, supermarkets, drug stores, direct mail, and book clubs. Home sales, the common route for encyclopedias, is yet another way to reach students outside the classroom.

It is easy to paint an exciting future for instructional materials outside the classroom. Basic, standardized school materials would be supplemented by an abundant supply of materials, from which child and parent could choose those that suit them best. The proliferation of nonschool materials could have its most significant impact in confronting the schools themselves with a new measure of competition. If nonschool markets grow, and if their materials prove attractive and effective, public schools may for the first time have to answer to parents for their choice of less effective materials. In the process, schools would be forced to clarify their standards for materials selection and might become more receptive to instructional techniques like those being used outside the school.

But this picture is too rosy. Although the deschooling of instructional materials need not await the deschooling of society, its chances of success remain speculative. Educational materials will probably seem too redundant, too great a luxury, to attract the number of private purchases necessary to support substantial research and development. And, as a matter of policy, it is hard to be enthusiastic about an instructional materials market that will characteristically exclude children whose parents are too poor or simply unwilling to invest in this new educational increment. At least for the near term, practice and policy suggest that schools will continue to be the main users and disseminators of instructional materials. Schools may respond to the challenge of nonschool materials not by adopting the new materials but by discrediting them. And acceptance, even if it occurs, will be in the usual small steps. The prospects for substantial change in the American schoolbook, inside the school or out, are evanescent, distant, and dim.

Appendix
Statutes Governing
Selection of Instructional
Materials

"Adoption" States

Alabama	Ala. Code §§ 16-36-01 to -10 (1975)
Alaska	Alaska Stat. § 14.07.050 (1975)
Arizona	Ariz. Rev. Stat. Ann. § 15-1101 (West Supp. 1977)
Arkansas	Ark. Stat. Ann. § 80-1703 (Supp. 1975)
Florida	Fla. Stat. Ann. § 233.16 (West 1977)
Georgia	Ga. Code Ann. § 32-707 (1976)
Indiana	Ind. Code § 20-10.1-9-1 (1976)
Kentucky	Ky. Rev. Stat. Ann. §§ 156.435, .445, .447 (Baldwin 1977)
Louisiana	La. Rev. Stat. Ann. § 17.7 (4) (West Supp. 1977)
Mississippi	Miss. Code Ann. § 37-43-31 (1972)
Nevada	Nev. Rev. Stat. § 390.140 (1973)
New Mexico	N.M. Stat. Ann. § 77-13-8 (Supp. 1975)
North Carolina	N.C. Gen. Stat. §§ 115-206.1-.2 (1975)
Oklahoma	Okla. Stat. Ann. tit. 70, § 16-102 (West Supp. 1977)
Oregon	Ore. Rev. Stat. § 337.050 (1975)
South Carolina	S.C. Code § 59-31-30 (1976)
Tennessee	Tenn. Code Ann. § 49-2008 (1977)
Texas	Tex. Educ. Code Ann. §§ 12.11-.16 (Vernon 1972)
Utah	Utah Code Ann. § 53-13-2 (1953)
Virginia	Va. Code § 22-296 (1973)
West Virginia	W. Va. Code § 18-2A-8 (1977)

"Nonadoption" States

California	Cal. Educ. Code § 9400 (West Supp. 1977)
Colorado	Colo. Const. art. 9, § 16
Connecticut	Conn. Gen. Stat. Ann. § 10-228 (West 1977)
Delaware	Del. Code Ann. tit. 15, § 122(b)(6) (1974)
Hawaii	Haw. Rev. Stat. § 296-36 (1968)
Idaho	Idaho Code § 33-118 (1963)
Illinois	Ill. Ann. Stat. ch. 122, § 28-6 (Smith-Hurd Supp. 1977)
Iowa	Iowa Code Ann. § 301.1 (West Supp. 1977)
Kansas	Kan. Stat. Ann. § 72-7513(a)(1) (Supp. 1976)
Maine	Me. Rev. Stat. Ann. tit. 20, §§ 161.7 (1964), 856 (Supp. 1976)
Maryland	Md. Ann. Code art. 77, §§ 67, 79 (1975)
Massachusetts	Mass. Gen. Laws Ann. ch. 71, § 48 (1971)
Michigan	Mich. Stat. Ann. §§ 15.41422, .41431 (1977)
Minnesota	Minn. Stat. Ann. § 123.35(2) (West 1960)
Missouri	Mo. Ann. Stat. § 170.051 (Vernon Supp. 1977)
Montana	Mont. Rev. Codes Ann. § 75-7603 (1947)
Nebraska	Neb. Rev. Stat. § 79-4, 118 (1976)
New Hampshire	N.H. Rev. Stat. Ann. § 189:16 (1964)
New Jersey	N.J. Stat. Ann. § 18A:34-1 (West 1968)
New York	N.Y. Educ. Law § 701 (McKinney Supp. 1976)
North Dakota	N.D. Cent. Code § 15-43-04 (1971)
Ohio	Ohio Rev. Code Ann. § 3329.08 (Page 1972)
Pennsylvania	Pa. Stat. Ann. tit. 24, § 8-801 (Purdon 1962)
Rhode Island	R.I. Gen. Laws §§ 16-1-9, 23-2 (1969)
South Dakota	S.D. Compiled Laws Ann. § 13-34-11 (1975)
Vermont	Vt. Stat. Ann. tit. 16, § 563(14) (1974)
Washington	Wash. Rev. Code Ann. § 28A.58.103 (Supp. 1977)

| Wisconsin | Wis. Stat. Ann. § 118.03 (West 1973) |
| Wyoming | Wyo. Stat. § 21.1-181 (Supp. 1975) |

Three states, Arizona, New Mexico and Arkansas, specify adoption procedures or constraints for materials used in elementary schools but not in high schools. Because this book is concerned with instructional materials in elementary schools, these have been classified as adoption states.

Notes

Chapter 1
Forces That Shape Instructional Materials

1. Governor's Commission on Public Education, Public Education in Texas (1969), cited in Kirst & Walker, *An Analysis of Curriculum Policy Making*, 41 Rev. of Ed. Res. 479, 492 (1971).

2. To Improve Learning: An Evaluation of Instructional Technology 84 (S. Tickton ed. 1970).

3. Publishers Weekly 14 (9 Dec. 1974).

4. Jencks, *Is the Public School Obsolete?* The Public Interest 18, 22 (Winter 1966).

5. Locke, *Has the Education Industry Lost Its Nerve?* Saturday Review 42 (16 Jan. 1971).

6. Ind. Const. art. 8, § 1.

7. Northshore School District No. 417 v. Kinnear, 84 Wash. 2d 685, 729, 530 P. 2d 178, 202 (1974).

8. Leeper v. State, 103 Tenn. 500, 53 S.W. 962 (1899).

9. 347 U.S. 483 (1954).

10. Loewen v. Turnipseed, Index No. GC 75-147-S (N.D. Miss.).

11. The discussion in this and the following paragraphs is drawn primarily from B. Sanderson & D. Kratochvil, Science—A Process Approach, Product Development Report No. 8 (1971) (ED-064-066), and Far West Laboratory for Educational Research and Development, Science—A Process Approach, Program Report, Elementary Science Information Unit (1970).

12. Gagné, *Psychological Issues in Science—A Process Approach*, in AASS Commission on Science Education, The Psychological Bases of Science—A Process Approach 1, 4 (1965).

13. Gagné, *The Individual Basis of Scientific Inquiry*, in *id.* 9, 12.

14. Science—A Process Approach, Part C, Measuring II, Temperature and Thermometers (1967).

15. *See generally* H. Cole, One Laboratory's Attempt at Transforming Educational Practice (1970) (ED-051-553).

16. Answer of defendant, Xerox Corp. and American Ass'n for Advancement of Science v. Sigma Scientific, Inc., Index No. 72 Civ. 954 R.O. (S.D.N.Y.).

Chapter 2
Instructional Technology: Past, Present, and Future

1. *See* Carpenter, History of American Schoolbooks 81 (1963); H. Minnich, William Holmes McGuffey and His Readers 57-58 (1936).

2. Publishers Weekly, 18 Dec. 1972, at 13, table iii.

3. Educational Media Producers Council, Annual Survey and Analysis of Educational Media Producers Sales 1972 (1973). These data were derived from known materials producers, all of whom "were invited to participate in this survey regardless of membership in the Council. . . . Based on detailed estimates of business done by nonreporting producers, including some 95 which responded in one or more earlier surveys, the reporting 103 producers' sales comprised about 88% of the total 1972 dollar volume shown for these products." *Id*. at i.

These figures reflect sales to educational institutions at all levels. Data by type for sales to elementary schools are scant and of questionable validity. Sales of all types of audiovisual materials to elementary schools represented 57% of the total audiovisual market in 1971 and 58.6% in 1972; the high school fraction rose from 33.7% to 34.2% during this period and the college fraction dropped from 9.3% to 7.2% *See* Educational Media Producers Council, Annual Survey and Analysis of Educational Media Producers Sales 1972, table 8, at 11.

4. Stolurow & Davis, *Teaching Machines and Computer-Based Systems*, in 2 Teaching Machines and Programmed Learning, Data and Directions 162, 168 (R. Glaser ed. 1965).

5. The research is summarized in Goldstein & Gotkin, *A Review of Research: Teaching Machines v. Programmed Textbooks as Presentation Modes*, 1 J. Programmed Instruction 29 (1962).

6. The discussion in this and the next two paragraphs is drawn from Atkinson, *CAI—Learning Aspects*, Computers and Education 11 (Gerard ed. 1967); Zinn, *Computer Technology for Teaching and Research on Instruction*, 37 Rev. of Ed. Res. 618 (1967); Suppes, *The Uses of Computers in Education* 215 Scient. Amer. 207 (1966).

7. S. Papert, *Teaching Children Thinking*, M.I.T., Artificial Intelligence Laboratory, LOGO Memo No. 2, 2-1 (October 1971); S. Papert, *Teaching Children to be Mathematicians vs. Teaching About Mathematics*, M.I.T., Artificial Intelligence Laboratory, LOGO Memo No. 4, 6 (July 1971); S. Papert, *Uses of Technology to Enhance Education*, M.I.T., Artificial Intelligence Laboratory, LOGO Memo No. 8, 48 (June 1973).

8. To Improve Learning: An Evaluation of Instructional Technology 75 (S. Tickton ed. 1970).

9. A range of estimates is presented in A. Oettinger, Run, Computer, Run, the Mythology of Educational Innovation 190-95 (1969).

10. J. Dewey, Democracy and Education: An Introduction to the Philosophy of Education 163 (paperback ed. 1966).

11. O. Handlin, John Dewey's Challenge to Education: Historical Perspectives on the Cultural Context 46 (1959). *See generally*, J. Dewey, Democracy and Education: An Introduction to the Philosophy of Education 164-170 (paperback ed. 1966).

12. Dyrli, *Is There Anything New About the New Science Textbooks?* Learning 30 (January 1976).

13. *See* Winn, *Change and Resistance to the New Social Studies*, 99 School and Society 182 (1971); Naylor, Can the New Social Studies Survive in the Public Schools? (Paper presented at the National Council for the Social Studies College and University Session, November 1973). *See generally*, L. Sikorski, A Study of the Current Status of the Implementation of Science and Mathematics Materials at the Pre-College Level in the Natural Sciences, Social Sciences, and Mathematics 14–46 (1976).

14. The discussion of IDP in this and the following paragraphs is drawn from B. Turnbull, L. Thorn & C. Hutchins, Promoting Change in Schools 151–64 (1974).

15. Joint Committee on Programmed Instruction and Teaching Machines, *Joint Committee Prepares Interim Guidelines*, 9 AV Comm. Rev. 206, 208 (1961).

16. *See, e.g.*, California State Dep't of Ed., An Instrument for the Qualitative Evaluation of Media Programs in California (1972).

17. Komoski, Statement Before Curriculum Development and Supplemental Materials Commission of the State of California, 11 July 1973 (mimeo).

18. Cal. Ed. Code § 9426.

19. Cal. Ed. Code § 9234.

20. Komoski, Statement Before Curriculum Development and Supplemental Materials Commission of the State of California, 11 July 1973 (mimeo).

21. *Compare* Cal. Ed. Code § 9263 *with* § 9600, which is more precisely drafted and applicable only to the adoption of high school textbooks.

22. California Dep't of Ed., Draft Preliminary Guidelines for Learner Verification (Jan. 1974).

23. Fla. Stats. Ann. § 233.25 (West Supp. 1975).

24. *See* Klein, Toward Consensus on Minimum Criteria for Educational Products 16 (1976).

Chapter 3
How Instructional Materials Are Purchased

1. Brickell, *State Organization for Educational Change: A Case Study and a Proposal*, in Innovation in Education 495–96 (M. Miles ed. 1964).

2. NIE Curriculum Development Task Force, Current Issues, Problems, and Concerns in Curriculum Development 3 (1976).

3. Cited in Kirst & Walker, *Curricular Decisions in the Political System*, in The Political Web of American Schools 202, 217 (F. Wirt & M. Kirst eds. 1972).

4. Kirst & Walker, *Curricular Decisions in the Political System*, in The Political Web of American Schools 202, 205–6 (F. Wirt & M. Kirst eds. 1972).

5. Kirst & Walker, *Curricular Decisions in the Political System*, in The Political Web of American Schools 202, 208-9 (F. Wirt & M. Kirst eds. 1972).

6. Cal. Ed. Code § 9202 (West Supp. 1974).

7. For the alignment of individual states, see Appendix.

8. Cal. Ed. Code § 9462 (West Supp. 1974).

9. This summary of the typical elements of local school organizations is drawn from Brickell, *supra* n.3 at 502-4.

10. Joint Committee of the National Education Ass'n and Ass'n of American Publishers, Selecting Instructional Materials for Purchase (1972).

11. Selection practices were observed in three school districts in western New York. One district was situated in the region's major city, another was in a suburb, and the third was in a rural area. The districts were located no more than thirty-five miles apart. Taken together, the three districts roughly embody the range of attributes present in school districts throughout New York state, with the exception of New York City. The information in this section is drawn from interviews with administrators and teachers in the three districts, and with publishers' sales representatives working in the districts.

12. Testimony Before the Sen. Educ. Comm., 8 Oct. 1974.

13. Cal. Ed. Code § 9402 (West Supp. 1974).

14. Aulie, *The Doctrine of Special Creation*, 34 Am. Bio. Teacher 191, 192 (April 1972).

15. *See generally, Creationists and Evolutionists: Confrontation in California*, 178 Science 724 (17 Nov. 1972); *Eden and Evolution*, 1 Saturday Rev. of Sciences 58-59 (Feb. 1973); *God and Darwin in California*, 17 Christianity Today 35 (22 Dec. 1972).

16. Quoted in *California's Evolution War: Should Genesis Get Equal Time?* 87 Christian Century 251, 252 (25 Feb. 1970).

17. Science Framework for California Schools 106 (1970).

18. *Creationists and Evolutionists: Confrontation in California*, 178 Science 724, 725 (17 Nov. 1972).

19. *See* Trillin, *A Public Hearing on the Origin of Species*, 48 New Yorker 55 (6 Jan. 1973); *God and Darwin in California*, 17 Christianity Today 35 (22 Dec. 1972).

20. *Creationists and Evolutionists: Confrontation in California*, 178 Science 724, 725 (17 Nov. 1972).

21. *Creationists and Evolutionists: Confrontation in California*, 178 Science 724, 725 (17 Nov. 1972).

22. *Board Will Decide Text Content*, Sacramento Bee, 10 Nov. 1972, § A, at 1, col. 4.

23. Layton, *Scientists Versus Fundamentalists: The California Compromise*, 54 Phi Delta Kappan 696 (June 1973); *Those Evolving Textbooks*, 17 Christianity Today 48 (5 Jan. 1963); *Creation Theory is Excluded from Texts*, Sacramento Bee, 15 Dec. 1972, § A, at 1, col. 2.

24. *Social Science Texts Will Include Creation Theory*, Sacramento Bee, 12 Jan. 1973, § A, at 3, col. 6; *Eden and Evolution*, 1 Saturday Rev. of Sciences 58 (Feb. 1973).

25. *State Board Delays Adopting Science Texts*, Sacramento Bee, 13 June 1975, § A, at 17, col. 1.

26. See Aulie, *The Doctrine of Special Creation*, 34 Amer. Bio. Teacher 191 (May 1972); *The Pressure to Rewrite Creation*, Business Week 184 (11 Nov. 1972); *Creationists and Evolutionists: Confrontation in California*, 178 Science 724 (17 Nov. 1972); *Creation's Role in Textbooks Promises A Lively Thursday Hearing*, Sacramento Bee, 5 Nov. 1972, § A, at 5, col. 1.

27. *California's Evolution War: Should Genesis Get Equal Time?* 87 Christian Century 252-53 (25 Feb. 1970).

28. *Creationists and Evolutionists: Confrontation in California*, 178 Science 724 (17 Nov. 1972); *Alternative Hypothesis* 227 Scientific American 43-44 (Aug. 1972); Layton, *Scientists versus Fundamentalists: The California Compromise*, 54 Phi Delta Kappan 696 (June 1973); *Divine Creationists Seek Equal School Texts Space*, Sacramento Bee, 30 March 1973, § A, at 4, col. 3.

29. Bredesen, *Anatomy of a Confrontation*, 23 J. of the Amer. Scientific Affiliation 146 (Dec. 1971); Layton, *Scientists versus Fundamentalists: The California Compromise*, 54 Phi Delta Kappan 696 (June 1973); *Biblical Creation Story Should Not be Forced into Science Textbooks*, Sacramento Bee, 16 Nov. 1972, § A, at 26, col. 1.

30. Report of Actions Taken by the State Board of Educ. 14-15 Sept. 1972.

31. See Bredesen, *Anatomy of a Confrontation*, 23 J. of Amer. Scientific Affiliation 146 (Dec. 1971); *State Board Okays Science Texts, May be Including Creation*, Sacramento Bee, 14 Dec. 1972, § B, at 1, col. 4; *The Pressure to Rewrite Creation*, Business Week 184-85 (11 Nov. 1972).

32. See T. van Geel, Authority to Control the School Program 129-35 (1976).

33. Tobias, *Teachers' Attitudes toward Programmed Instructional Terms*, 2 J. of Programmed Instruction 25 (1963). Tobias, *Lack of Knowledge and Fear of Automation as Factors in Teachers' Attitudes toward Programmed Instruction and Other Media*, 14 AV Comm. Rev. 99 (1966); Tobias, *Dimensions of Teachers' Attitudes toward Instructional Media*, 5 Am. Educ. Res. J. 91 (1968).

34. *See, e.g.*, Latham, *Measuring Teacher Responses to Instructional Materials*, in A Sourcebook for the Evaluation of Instructional Materials and Media 221 (Armstrong ed. 1973); McClure, A Pilot Project on Users' Needs and Teacher Inservice Education Products (Far West Laboratory for Educational Research & Development, 1976).

35. Quoted in Klein, Toward a Consensus on Minimum Criteria for Educational Products 18-19 (1976).

36. *See generally* D. Rafky & M. Beckerman, Teachers' Acceptance of Innovations: Self-Interest, Altruism, and Professionalization (ED–079–267) (1971).

37. *See, e.g.*, Stern & Keislar, Teacher Attitudes and Attitude Change 56 (ED–109–072) (1975).

38. R. Carlson, Adoption of Educational Innovations 83 (1965).

39. Dodge, *et. al.*, *How Teachers Perceive Media*, Educ. Tech. 21 (1974).

40. Dawson, *Teacher Militancy and Instructional Media*, 19 AV Comm. Rev. 184, 190, 195-96 (1971).

41. *See* R. Carlson, Adoption of Educational Innovations 9 (1965); T. Baldridge, The Impact of Individuals, Organizational Structure, and Environment on Organizational Innovation, Research and Development 25, Memo No. 124, Stanford Center for Research and Development in Teaching (1974).

Chapter 4
How Instructional Materials Are Produced

1. Except where otherwise noted, the discussion in this section is based on H. Black, The American Schoolbook (1967); Brammer, *Textbook Publishing*, in What Happens in Book Publishing 320 (C. Grannis ed. 1967); Educational Products Information Exchange Institute, Textbooks—Recent Review and a Look at the Industry (1970); Institute for Educational Development, Research and Development in the Educational Materials Industries (1969).

2. 1973 10-K Report of Harcourt Brace Jovanovich, Inc.

3. H. Black, The American Schoolbook 60-61 (1967).

4. H. Black, The American Schoolbook 60-61 (1967).

5. Brammer, *Textbook Publishing*, in What Happens in Book Publishing 320-32 (C. Grannis ed. 1967).

6. "The School Department of Harcourt Brace Jovanovich, which also publishes traditional textbooks, at times ventures into innovative publishing. It published the first high school textbook to use programmed instruction (*English 2600*), the first elementary school English series to use generative transformational grammar (*The Roberts English Series*), and, in 1970, a praiseworthy elementary school social studies series (*Social Science: Concepts and Values*). Educational Products Information Exchange Institute, Textbooks—Recent Reviews and a Look at the Industry 8 (1970).

7. Institute for Educational Development, Research and Development in the Educational Materials Industries 32 (1969).

8. N.Y. Times, 20 Nov. 1965, at 55, col. 8.

9. N.Y. Times, 11 Jan. 1966, at 41, col. 2.

10. Doebler, *Multimedia Moves Ahead Fast in Educational Publishing*, Publishers Weekly 40, 42 (21 May 1973).

11. Doebler, *Multimedia Moves Ahead Fast in Educational Publishing*, Publishers Weekly 42 (21 May 1973).

12. Institute for Educational Development, Research and Development in the Educational Materials Industries (1969).

13. The textbook figure, drawn from a survey of firm descriptions in *Literary Marketplace* (1975), includes publishers of elementary school materials that may also produce secondary school materials and other educational materials but excludes any publisher not listed as producing elementary grade materials.

The nontext figure, which includes text publishers that also produce nontext materials, is drawn exclusively from the membership directories of the two predominant trade organizations, the Educational Media Producers Council and the National Audio-Visual Association, and may therefore be understated.

14. Total book publishing industry sales in 1967, 1970, and 1971 were approximately $2.38 billion, $2.922 billion, and $3.083 billion respectively. Though estimated from reports of the Association of American Publishers, these figures are roughly comparable with those compiled by the Bureau of the Census. The *Census of Manufactures* reports $2,255,300,000 total receipts for 1967, and shipments valued at $2,677,000,000 for 1970 and $2,814,100,000 for 1971.

The portions of these sales attributable to textbook and standardized test sales at all levels, elementary through college, were as follows:

1967: $729,350,000—31% of total publishing revenues

1970: $865,610,000—30% of total publishing revenues

1971: $903,070,000—29% of total publishing revenues

Sales of text materials exclusively for grades K–8 can be narrowed further to:

1967: $265,610,000—36% of total text revenues and 11% of total publishing revenues

1970: $301,210,000—35% of total text revenues and 10% of total publishing revenues

1971: $314,040,000—35% of total text revenues and 10% of total publishing revenues

Publishers Weekly 13, table iii (18 Dec. 1972).

Comparable Bureau of the Census textbook figures for these years are $733.6 million total receipts for 1967, and $815.9 million and $846.8 million value of product shipments in 1970 and 1971 respectively.

15. Association of American Publishers, 1973 Statistics on ELHI Publishing Industry, Table T-1 (1974).

Total sales to all grade levels of audiovisual materials, including films, filmstrips, slides, records, tapes, multimedia kits and related products, were $119.2 million in 1967, $166.1 million in 1970, and $193.7 million in 1971. Educational Media Producers Council, Annual Survey and Analysis of Educational Media Producers Sales, 1972, Table 1 (1973). These figures, which appear to be the most accurate available, depart only slightly from the totals employed in the AAP combined data, of $119 million (1967); $164 million (1970) and $194 million (1971), which are derived from the EMPC data. *See* Association of American Publishers, 1973 Statistics on ELHI Publishing Industry (1974).

The figures represent sales to consumers other than schools and colleges—to libraries, business and industry, government agencies, and religious institutions. These nonschool purchases account, however, for only about 10% of the aggregate. Educational Media Producers Council, Annual Survey and Analysis of Educational Media Producers' Sales 1972, Table 9 (1973).

16. D. Quirk, The El-Hi Market 1975–1980: Instructional Materials for Elementary and High Schools 81–82 (1974).

17. *See* D. Vanier, Market Structure and the Business of Book Publishing 13 (1973).

18. R. Nelson, M. Peck, E. Kalachek, Technology, Economic Growth and Public Policy 67 (1967); Mansfield, *Size of Firm, Market Structure, and Innovation*, 71 J. Pol. Econ. 556 (1963); Mansfield, *Industrial Research and Development Expenditures: Determinants, Prospects, and Relation to Size of Firm and Inventive Output*, 72 J. Pol. Econ. 319 (1964); Markham, *Market Structure, Business Conduct and Innovation*, 55 Am. Econ. Rev. 323 (1965); Schmookler, *Bigness, Fewness, and Research*, 67 J. Pol. Econ. 628 (1959).

The precise role of scale economies is conjectural, although it does seem clear that one reason for the difference lies in the greater likelihood that a structured program of research and development will be found in the large rather than small firms, a fact that will naturally skew any comparison of average firm investment toward a finding of greater proportional investment among larger firms.

19. This phenomenon may help to explain the finding of some historical studies analyzing the sources of significant inventions and suggesting that more of these inventions stem from individual or small-scale efforts than from large-scale corporate endeavors. *See generally* J. Jewkes, D. Sawers & R. Stillerman, The Sources of Invention (1969).

20. The discussion in this and the following paragraph is drawn from Mueller, *A Case Study of Product Discovery and Innovation Costs*, 24 So. Econ. J. 80 (1957).

21. Bureau of the Census, 1967 Census of Manufacturers, Concentration Ratios in Manufacturing, Part 2, table 6 (1971).

22. D. Quirk, The El-Hi Market 1975-1980: Instructional Materials for Elementary and High Schools 25, 81–82 (1974).

Because these concentration ratios focus down no more narrowly than the kindergarten through high school market, they do not necessarily present an accurate picture of conditions in the narrower K-8 industry. On the figures, a highly concentrated K-8 submarket is not necessarily inconsistent with a moderately concentrated elhi market, for the submarkets could be segmented by producers, with some accounting for all K-8 sales and others for all high school sales. To take the most extreme case, if all K-8 sales were made by the firms with the largest elhi market shares, the four largest companies would in 1970 have accounted for 42% of K-8 sales, the eight largest 74%, and the ten largest 85%. These figures were derived by adjusting the 1970 sales figure of $411,210,000 for K-8 instructional materials, drawn from EMPC and AAP sources, to the higher basis implicit in the Knowledge Industry Publications elhi sales figure of $900,907,430 for 1970. The 1970 elhi sales figure derived from EMPC and AAP sources was $641,050,000, so the following ratio was employed:

$411,210,000 (AAP/EMPC–K-8) : x(KIP)–K-8) =

$$\$641,050,000 \,(\text{AAP/EMPC–elhi}) : \$900,907,430 (\text{KIP–elhi})$$

This equation yields a KIP–K-8 figure of $577,900,000. This adjustment arbitrarily assumes that the divergence between AAP/EMPC and KIP elhi figures applies also to K-8 figures from the two sets of sources.

Using an adjusted AAP/EMPC K-8 sales figure of $411,410,000 as the basis for deriving shares based on the KIP sales figures for each firm, the four largest firms would have a 59% market share, the seven largest firms 95%, and the eight largest firms 100%. In fact, the instructional materials industry is not this segmented. The available, more impressionistic, data suggest that conditions in the K-8 segment of the industry approximate those in the elhi segment generally.

However, "if the textbook market alone is considered, the degree of concentration becomes considerably greater. Here the largest firm, Scott, Foresman, has about 18% of the domestic market, and the five largest publishers have over 60%. This is more concentrated than hardcover trade publishing, but less concentrated than paperback, reference or college textbook publishing." D. Quirk, the El-Hi Market 1975-1980: Instructional Materials for Elementary and High Schools, 82–83, 96–153 (1974).

23. D. Quirk, The El-Hi Market 1975-1980: Instructional Materials for Elementary and High Schools, 82-83, 96-153 (1974).

24. Standard and Poor's 1965 Industry Survey, Basic Analysis, Publishing, at 31.

25. Comanor, *Research and Competitive Product Differentiation in the Pharmaceutical Industry in the United States*, 31 Economica 372 (1964) is the source for the findings referred to here.

26. Turner, *The Patent System and Competitive Policy*, 44 N.Y.U. L. Rev. 450, 457 (1969).

27. 101 U.S. 99 (1879).

28. *See* 37 C.F.R. § 202.1(c) (1975).

29. Brown Instrument Co. v. Warner, 161 F.2d 910 (D.C. Cir. 1947).

30. *See, e.g.*, Norton Printing Co. v. Augustana Hospital, 155 U.S.P.Q. 133 (N.D. Ill. 1967).

31. 329 F. Supp. 517 (S.D.N.Y. 1971).

32. Morrissey v. Procter & Gamble Co., 379 F.2d 675, 678-679 (1st Cir. 1967).

33. Continental Cas. Co. v. Beardsley, 253 F.2d 702, 706 (2d Cir. 1958).

34. This level of product differentiation could be avoided in a market that encouraged licenses and cross-licenses between a copyright proprietor and his competitors. These networks of permission have not developed, however, presumably because of the low level of investment required to distinguish one work's expression from another's.

35. Hearings Before the Subcomm. on Patents, Trademarks and Copyrights of the Sen. Comm. on the Judiciary, Pursuant to S. Res. 56 on S. 1361, 93rd Cong. 1st Sess., 184, 185, 187 (1973).

36. S. 22 § 107, 94th Cong. 1st Sess. (1975).

37. 487 F.2d 1345 (Ct. Claims 1973), *aff'd by an equally divided court*, 95 S. Ct. 1344 (1975).

38. 409 U.S. 63 (1972).

39. 15 U.S. (How.) 62 (1853).

40. 126 U.S. 1 (1888).

41. 59 U.S.P.Q. 342 (P.O. Bd. Apps. 1943).

42. 29 F.2d 784, 785 (W.D. Pa. 1928).

43. 112 U.S.P.Q. 439 (P.O. Bd. Apps. 1955).

44. 210 F. 443 (6th Cir. 1913).

45. In re Miller, 164 U.S.P.Q. 46 (C.C.P.A. 1969).

46. In re Royka & Martin, 180 U.S.P.Q. 580, 583 (C.C.P.A. 1974).

47. 184 U.S.P.Q. 309 (S.D. Fla. 1974).

48. Restatement, Torts § 747, Comment (b)(f), (1939).

Chapter 5
Subsidies to Innovation in Instructional Materials

1. Cooperative Research Act, Pub. L. No. 531, 68 Stat. 533 (1954) (repealed 1975); National Defense Education Act of 1958, Pub. L. No. 85-864,

§§ 701, 731, 72 Stat. 1595 (20 U.S.C. §§ 541, 551 [1970]); Elementary and Secondary Education Act of 1965, Pub. L. No. 89-10, 79 Stat. 27 *et seq.* (20 U.S.C. § 236 *et seq.* [1970 & Supp. 1977]); Education Amendments of 1972, Pub. L. No. 92-318, Title III, § 301(a)(2), 86 Stat. 326 (20 U.S.C. §§ 1221a, 1221e [1970 & Supp. 1977]).

2. P. Greenwood *et. al.*, 3 Federal Programs Supporting Educational Change 34 (1975).

3. The discussion in this and the following four paragraphs is based on a review of letters and recent annual reports from forty-four private foundations which responded to a request for information sent to the fifty-eight private foundations reported by the 1975 Educational Media Yearbook as having awarded grants to some phase of instructional materials research and development.

4. National Science Foundation Curriculum Development and Implementation for Pre-College Science Education, Report Prepared for the House Comm. on Science and Technology 94th Cong. 1st Sess. 195 (1975). (Hereinafter cited as Curriculum Report.).

5. National Science Foundation Act of 1950, Pub. L. No. 507, § 3(a)(1), 64 Stat. 149 (42 U.S.C. § 1862(d) [1970]).

6. The discussion in this and the following paragraphs draws substantially on Curriculum Report 108-9, 159, 162, 166, 169, 184-87, 189-90.

7. *See* National Science Foundation, Course and Curriculum Improvement Projects 5 (1974).

8. National Science Foundation, Division of Pre-College Education in Science, Leadership Specialist Directory 3 (1975).

9. *See* Curriculum Report 304; Nelkin, *The Science-Textbook Controversies*, 234 Scient. Amer. 33-39 (1976).

10. Curriculum Report 5.

11. 20 U.S.C. § 453(a)(1) (1970).

12. Strengthening Instruction in Academic Subjects, Title III, Part A, National Defense Education Act as Amended, Annual Report: Fiscal Year 1972, 27, 36, Table 4, 37, Table 5 (1973) (ERIC No. ED-082-382).

13. H.R. 16572, 92d Cong. 2d Sess. (11 Sept. 1972); H.R. 4916, 92d Cong. 1st Sess. (25 Feb. 1971).

14. Hearings Before the Select Subcomm. on Education of the House Comm. on Education and Labor on H.R. 4916 92d Cong. 2d Sess. 15 (1972).

15. R. Filep, The Impact of Research on Utilization of Media for Educational Purposes 11, 46, 174-75 (1970).

16. Sen. Comm. on Labor and Public Welfare, 88th Cong. 1st Sess. Hearings.

17. Discussion in this and the next three paragraphs is drawn from R. Filep, The Impact of Research on Utilization of Media for Educational Purposes 12-14, 49, 139-74 (1970).

18. *See generally* R. Dershimer, The Federal Government and Educational R&D 29–83 (1976).

19. Pub. L. 85–864, Title XI § 1101, as added Pub. L. 88–665, Title IX § 901(a), 16 Oct. 1964, 78 Stat. 1107.

20. R. Filep, The Impact of Research on Utilization of Media for Educational Purposes 152 (1970).

21. *See* M. Tucker *et. al.*, Building Capacity for Renewal and Reform: An Initial Report on Knowledge Production and Utilization in Education 10–11 (1973) (ED–087–095).

22. Baldridge & Johnson, The Impact of Educational R&D Centers and Laboratories: An Analysis of Effective Organizational Strategies 55–57 (1972).

23. M. Tucker *et. al.*, Building Capacity for Renewal and Reform: An Initial Report on Knowledge Production and Utilization in Education 9–10 (1973) (ED–087–095).

24. *See* L. Hoehn, The Regional Educational Laboratories as Change Agents 42–43 (University Microfilms 1967).

25. U.S. Office of Education, Division of Education Laboratories, Bureau of Research, A Progress Report on the Twenty Education Laboratories 1 (1967).

26. The discussion in this and the following four paragraphs is drawn primarily from L. Hoehn, The Regional Educational Laboratories as Change Agents 50–54, 174, 140 (University Microfilms 1967).

27. Office of Education, Focus on Innovation: A Report on the Status and Operation of ESEA Title III, Fiscal Year 1969, 55 (1971).

28. H. Cole, One Laboratory's Attempt at Transforming Educational Practice 9–11 (1970) (ED–051–553).

29. C.L. Hutchins, Far West Laboratory for Educational Research and Development, Educational Development Case Study: An Elementary Science Information Unit iii–v (1971).

30. L. Hoehn, The Regional Educational Laboratories as Change Agents 155 (University Microfilm 1967).

31. B. Turnbull *et. al.*, Promoting Change in Schools 135–36 (1974); Baldridge & Johnson, The Impact of Educational R&D Centers and Laboratories: An Analysis of Effective Organizational Strategies 59 (1972).

32. In L. Hoehn, The Regional Educational Laboratories as Change Agents 164 (University Microfilms 1967).

33. The discussion in this and the next two paragraphs is primarily drawn from S. Bailey & E. Mosher, ESEA: The Office of Education Administers a Law 89, 373 (1968).

34. R. Dershimer, The Federal Government and Educational R&D 83–89 (1976).

35. S. Bailey & E. Mosher, ESEA: The Office of Education Administers a Law 96 (1968).

36. Message on Education Reform to U.S. Congress, by President Richard M. Nixon 6-7 (3 March 1970), in Weekly Compilation of Presidential Documents 307 (9 March 1970).

37. *See* R. Levien, National Institute of Education: Preliminary Plan for the Proposed Institute 39-40 (1971); NIE, Office of Public Information, N.I.E.: Its History and Programs 32-34 (1974); National Institute of Education, Fiscal Year 1974 Supplemental Budget Justification 48-50.

38. Letter of June 3, 1973 from Robert T. Filep, National Center for Educational Technology, incorporated in 21 June 1973 memorandum to NAVA Legislative Committee from Kenton Pattie, Vice President and Educational Director, National Audio-Visual Association, Inc.

39. National Institute of Education, ERIC Fact Sheet, October 1976.

40. Final Report of Consultants to the Director and the National Council on Educational Research, R&D Funding Policies of the National Institute of Education: Review and Recommendations 35-37 (1975).

41. R. Levien, National Institute of Education: Preliminary Plan for the Proposed Institute 37 (1971).

42. Final Report of Consultants to the Director and the National Council on Educational Research, R&D Funding Policies of the National Institute of Education: Review and Recommendations 36-38 (1975).

Chapter 6
New Paths for Research, Development, and Dissemination

1. T. van Geel, Authority to Control the School Program 169 (1976).

2. S. 1480, 94th Cong. 1st Sess., 120 Cong. Rec. 6226 (1975).

3. *See* I.R.C. § 174. *But see* Treas. Reg. § 1.174-2(a) (1974); Rev. Rul. 73-395.

4. *See generally* Cary, *Copyright Registration and Computer Programs*, 11 Bull. Copyr. Soc. 362 (1964).

5. 17 U.S.C. § 102(a) (1978).

6. 17 U.S.C. § 102(b) (1978).

7. *See, e.g.*, Application of Johnston, 502 F.2d 765 (C.C.P.A. 1974), *rev'd sub. nom.* Dann v. Johnston, 425 U.S. 219 (1976).

8. *See* Gottschalk v. Benson, 409 U.S. 63 (1972).

9. *See generally* Report of the President's Commission on the Patent System, To Promote the Progress of Useful Arts 12-13 (1966).

10. *See* Galbi, *Proposal for New Legislation to Protect Computer Programming*, 17 Bull. Copyr. Soc. 280 (1970). *See generally* Kindermann, *Special Protection Systems for Computer Programs—A Comparative Study*, 7 Int. Rev. of Indus. Prop. & Copyr. Law 301 (1976).

11. The discussion in this and the following paragraph is based on Galbi, *Proposal for New Legislation to Protect Computer Programming*, 17 Bull. Copyr. Soc. 280 (1970).

12. *See, e.g.*, Leontief, *On Assignment of Patent Rights on Inventions Made Under Government Research Contracts*, 77 Harv. L. Rev. 492, 495 (1964).

13. Except where otherwise indicated, the discussion in this and the following four paragraphs is drawn from National Science Foundation, Curriculum Development and Implementation for Pre-College Science Education, Report Prepared for the House Comm. on Science and Technology, 94th Cong. 1st Sess. Serial Q (November 1975); National Science Foundation, Policies for the Distribution of Publications and Other Materials Developed Under the Science Education Programs of the National Science Foundation (14 February 1975).

14. 45 C.F.R. § 650.11 (1976).

15. 45 C.F.R. § § 650.8(c); 650.9(c)(1) (1976).

16. 30 Fed. Reg. 9408 (12 July 1965).

17. 35 Fed. Reg. 7317 (9 May 1970). Except where otherwise indicated, the discussion in this and the following three paragraphs is drawn from 35 Fed. Reg. 7317-7320 (9 May 1970).

18. For background on legislative efforts in this area, there is probably no better source than the publications of the State Education Accountability Repository, the research arm of the Cooperative Accountability Project, a seven-state project initiated in April 1972 with funds from ESEA and with Colorado as the administering state.

19. Mich. Stats. Ann. § 15.2085(11)(1)(a) (1975).

20. Fla. Stat. Ann. § 229.57(2)(b) (1977).

21. Cal. Ed. Code § 13487 (1977 Supp.).

22. 60 Cal. App. 3d 814, 131 Cal. Rptr. 854 (1st Dist. 1976) *hearing denied*, 29 Sept. 1976. *See generally* Sugarman, *Accountability Through the Courts*, 82 School Rev. 233 (1974).

23. Cal. Ed. Code § 10759; Cal. Admin. Code § § 435-36 (State Off. Admin. Procedure 1970).

24. Cal. Ed. Code § 8505.

25. Cal. Ed. Code § 7504.

26. Discussion in this and the following two paragraphs is based on J. Mecklenburger, Performance Contracting in the Schools: Profit Motive Tested as Incentive to Learning (1972); G. Hall & N. Rapp, Four Case Studies in Educational Performance Contracting (Rand Corp. R-900/4 HEW December 1971).

27. G. Hall & N. Rapp, Four Case Studies in Educational Performance Contracting VI (Rand Corp. R-900/4 HEW December 1971).

28. G. Hall & N. Rapp, Four Case Studies in Educational Performance Contracting 12 (Rand Corp. R-900/4 HEW December 1971).

29. D. Weiler, A Public School Voucher Demonstration: The First Year at Alum Rock IV (Rand Corp. 1974).

30. National Institute of Education, Education Vouchers: The Experience at Alum Rock II (1973).

31. *See generally* Areen, *Education Vouchers*, 6 Harv. C.R.-C.L. Law Rev. 466 (1971); *Education Vouchers: The Fruit of the Lemon Tree*, 24 Stan. L. Rev. 687 (1972).

32. *See generally* McCann, *The Politics and Ironies of Educational Change: The Case of Vouchers*, 2 Yale Rev. of Law and Soc. Action 374 (1972).

Bibliography

Published Materials

"Alternative Hypothesis." *Scientific American*, August 1972, pp. 43–44.

American Association for the Advancement of Science. *Science–A Process Approach: Part C, Measuring II, Temperature and Thermometers*. New York: Xerox Corporation, 1967.

Areen, Judith. "Education Vouchers." *Harvard Civil Rights–Civil Liberties Law Review* 6(1971):466–504.

Association of American Publishers. *1973 Statistics on ELHI Publishing Industry*. Washington, D.C.: National Education Association, 1974.

Atkinson, Richard C. "CAI: Learning Aspects." In *Computers and Education*, edited by R.W. Gerard. New York: McGraw-Hill, 1967.

Aulie, Richard P. "The Doctrine of Special Creation." *American Biology Teacher*, May 1972, pp. 191–200.

Bailey, Stephen K., and Mosher, Edith K. *ESEA: The Office of Education Administers a Law*. Syracuse: Syracuse University Press, 1968.

Bedingfield, Robert E. "Time and G.E. Plan Educational Unit." *New York Times*, 20 November 1965, p. 45.

"Biblical Creation Story Should not be Forced into Science Textbooks." *Sacramento Bee*, 6 November 1972.

Black, Hillel. *The American Schoolbook*. New York: Morrow, 1967.

"Board will Decide Text Content." *Sacramento Bee*, 10 November 1972.

"Book Sales 1971: A Modest Growth." *Publishers Weekly*, 18 December 1972, pp. 12–14.

Brammer, Mauck. "Textbook Publishing." In *What Happens in Book Publishing*, 2d ed., edited by Chandler B. Grannis, pp. 320–332. New York: Columbia University Press, 1967.

Bredesen, Harold. "Anatomy of a Confrontation." *Journal of the American Scientific Affiliation*, December 1971, pp. 146–49.

Brickell, Henry M. "State Organization for Educational Change: A Case Study and a Proposal." In *Innovation in Education*, edited by Matthew B. Miles. New York: Columbia University, Teachers College Press, 1964.

Bureau of the Census. "Concentration Ratios." In *1967 Census of Manufacturers*. Washington, D.C.: Government Printing Office, 1971.

California State Department of Education. *An Instrument for the Qualitative Evaluation of Media Programs in California*. Sacramento: California State Department of Education, 1972.

Carlson, Richard O. *Adoption of Educational Innovations*. Eugene, Ore.: Center for the Advanced Study of Educational Administration, 1965.

Carpenter, Charles. *History of American Schoolbooks*. Philadelphia: University of Pennsylvania Press, 1963.

Cary, George D. "Copyright Registration and Computer Programs." *Bulletin of the Copyright Society* 11(1964):362-68.

Chandler, Russell. "Those Evolving Textbooks." *Christianity Today*, 5 January 1973, pp. 48-49.

Comanor, William S. "Research and Competitive Product Differentiation in the Pharmaceutical Industry in the United States." *Economica* 31(1964):372-84.

"Creation's Role in Textbooks Promises a Lively Thursday Hearing," *Sacramento Bee*, 5 November 1972.

"Creation Theory is Excluded from Texts." *Sacramento Bee*, 15 December 1972.

Dawson, Paul. "Teacher Militancy and Instructional Media." *AV Communication Review* 19(1971):184-97.

Dershimer, Richard A. *The Federal Government and Educational R&D*. Lexington, Mass.: D.C. Heath, Lexington Books, 1976.

Dewey, John. *Democracy and Education: An Introduction to the Philosophy of Education*. Riverside, N.J.: Free Press, 1966.

"Divine Creationists Seek Equal School Texts Space." *Sacramento Bee*, 30 March 1973.

Dodge, Martin; Bogdan, Robert; Brogden, Nancy; and Lewis, Richard. "How Teachers Perceive Media." *Educational Technology*, January 1974, pp. 21-24.

Doebler, Paul. "Multimedia Moves Ahead Fast in Educational Publishing." *Publishers Weekly*, 21 May 1973, pp. 40-43.

Dyrli, Odvard Egil. "Is There Anything New About the New Science Textbooks?" *Learning*, January 1976, pp. 30-35.

"Eden and Evolution." *Saturday Review of the Sciences*, February 1973, pp. 58-59.

Educational Media Producers Council. *Annual Survey and Analysis of Educational Media Producers Sales, 1972*. Fairfax, Va.: Educational Media Producers Council, 1972.

Educational Products Information Exchange Institute. *Textbooks—Recent Reviews and a Look at the Industry*. New York: Educational Products Exchange Institute, 1970.

"Education Vouchers: The Fruit of the Lemon Tree." *Stanford Law Review* 24(1972):687-711.

Far West Laboratory for Educational Research and Development. *Science—A Process Approach: Program Report, Elementary Science Information Unit*. New York: Xerox Education Division, 1970.

Forbes, Cheryl. "God and Darwin in California." *Christianity Today*, 22 December 1972, pp. 35-36.

Gagné, Robert M. "The Individual Basis of Scientific Inquiry." In *The Psychological Bases of Science–A Process Approach*, edited by AAAS Commission on Science Education, pp. 9-25. Washington, D.C.: American Association for the Advancement of Science, 1965.

———. "Psychological Issues in Science–A Process Approach." In *The Psychological Bases of Science–A Process Approach*, edited by AAAS Commission on Science Education, pp. 1-8. Washington, D.C.: American Association for the Advancement of Science, 1965.

Galbi, Elmer. "Proposal for New Legislation to Protect Computer Programming." *Bulletin of the Copyright Society* 17(1970):280-96.

van Geel, Tyll. *Authority to Control the School Program*. Lexington, Mass.: D.C. Heath, Lexington Books, 1976.

Goldstein, Leo S. and Gotkin, Lassar G. "A Review of Research: Teaching Machines v. Programmed Textbooks as Presentation Modes." *Journal of Programed Instruction* 1(1962):29-36.

Governor's Committee on Public Education. *Public Education in Texas*. Austin, Texas: Texas Education Agency, 1969.

Greenwood, Peter W.; Mann, Dale; and McLaughlin, Milbrey. *Federal Programs Supporting Educational Change III: The Process of Change*. Santa Monica, Calif.: Rand Corporation, 1975.

Hall, George R., and Rapp, N. *Four Case Studies in Educational Performance Contracting*. Vol. 6. Santa Monica, Calif.: Rand Corporation, 1971.

Handlin, Oscar. *John Dewey's Challenge to Education: Historical Perspectives on the Cultural Context*. Westport, Conn.: Greenwood Press, 1959.

Jencks, Christopher. "Is the Public School Obsolete?" *The Public Interest*, Winter 1966, pp. 18-27.

Jewkes, John; Sawers, David; and Stillerman, Richard. *The Sources of Invention*. 2d ed. New York: Norton, 1969.

Joint Committee of the National Education Association and Association of American Publishers. *Selecting Instructional Materials for Purchase*. Washington, D.C.: National Education Association, 1972.

Joint Committee on Programmed Instruction and Teaching Machines. "Joint Committee Prepares Interim Guidelines." *AV Communication Review* 9(1961):206-208.

Kindermann, Manfred. "Special Protection Systems for Computer Programs– A Comparative Study." *International Review of Industrial Property and Copyright Law* 7(1976):301-31.

Kirst, Michael W., and Walker, Decker F. "An Analysis of Curriculum Policy Making." *Review of Educational Research* 41(1971):479-509.

———. "Curricular Decisions in the Political System." In *The Political Web of American Schools*, edited by Frederick Wirt and Michael Kirst. Boston: Little, Brown, 1972.

Larsen, Rebecca. "California's Evolution War: Should Genesis get Equal Time?" *Christian Century*, 25 February 1970, pp. 251-53.

Layton, Donald H. "Scientists Versus Fundamentalists: The California Compromise." *Phi Delta Kappan* 54(1973):696-97.

Leontief, Wassily. "On Assignment of Patent Rights on Inventions Made Under Government Research Contracts." *Harvard Law Review* 77(1964):492-97.

Levien, Roger E. *National Institute of Education: Preliminary Plan for the Proposed Institute*. Santa Monica, Calif.: Rand Corporation, 1971.

Literary Marketplace. New York: Bowker, 1975.

Locke, Robert W. "Has the Education Industry Lost its Nerve?" *Saturday Review*, 16 January 1971, p. 42.

McCann, Walter, "The Politics and Ironies of Educational Change: The Case of Vouchers." *Yale Review of Law and Social Action* 2(1972):374-89.

Mansfield, Edwin. "Industrial Research and Development Expenditures: Determinants, Prospects, and Relation to Size of Firm and Inventive Output." *Journal of Political Economy* 72(1964):319-40.

_____. "Size of Firm, Market Structure, and Innovation." *Journal of Political Economy*, 71(1963):556-76.

Markham, Jesse W. "Market Structure, Business Conduct and Innovation." *American Economic Review* 55(1965):323-32.

Maryles, Daisy. "U.S. Official Backs Parents in Textbooks Dispute." *Publishers Weekly*, 9 December 1974, p. 14.

Mecklenburger, James A. *Performance Contracting in the Schools: Profit Motive Tested as Incentive to Learning*. Arlington, Va.: National School of Public Relations Association, 1972.

Minnich, Harvey C. *William Holmes McGuffey and His Readers*. New York: American Book, 1936.

Mueller, Willard F. "A Case Study of Product Discovery and Innovation Costs." *Southern Economic Journal* 24(1957):80-86.

National Institute of Education. *Education Vouchers: The Experience at Alum Rock*. Vol. 2. Washington, D.C.: National Institute of Education, 1973.

_____. *N.I.E.: Its History and Programs*. Washington, D.C.: National Institute of Education, 1974.

National Science Foundation. *Course and Curriculum Improvement Projects*. Washington, D.C.: National Science Foundation, 1974.

_____. *Leadership Specialist Directory*. Washington, D.C.: National Science Foundation, 1975.

Nelkin, Dorothy, "The Science-Textbook Controversies." *Scientific American*, April 1976, pp. 33-39.

Nelson, Richard R.; Peck, Merton J.; and Kalachek, Edward D. *Technology, Economic Growth and Public Policy*. Washington, D.C.: Brookings Institution, 1967.

Oettinger, Anthony G. *Run, Computer, Run: The Mythology of Educational Innovation.* Cambridge, Mass.: Harvard University Press, 1969.

"The Pressure to Rewrite Creation." *Business Week*, 11 November 1972, pp. 184–86.

Quirk, Dantia. *The El-Hi Market 1975-1980: Instructional Materials for Elementary and High Schools.* White Plains, N.Y.: Knowledge Industry Publications, 1974.

Report of the President's Commission on the Patent System. *To Promote the Progress of Useful Arts.* Washington, D.C.: Government Printing Office, 1967.

Schmookler, Jacob. "Bigness, Fewness, and Research." *Journal of Political Economy*, 67(1959):628–35.

Smith, Gene. "R.C.A. Confirms Random House Bid." *New York Times*, 11 January 1966, p. 35.

"Social Science Texts Will Include Creation Theory." *Sacramento Bee*, 12 January 1973.

Standard and Poor's 1965 Industry Survey: Basic Analysis, Publishing. New York: Standard and Poor's Corporation, 1965.

"State Board Delays Adopting Science Texts." *Sacramento Bee*, 13 June 1975.

"State Board Okays Science Texts, May be Including Creation," *Sacramento Bee*, 14 December 1972.

Stolurow, Lawrence M., and Davis, Daniel. "Teaching Machines and Computer-Based Systems." In *Teaching Machines and Programmed Learning II: Data and Directions*, edited by Robert Glaser, pp. 162-212. Washington, D.C.: Association for Educational Communications and Technology, 1965.

Sugarman, Stephen D. "Accountability Through the Courts." *School Review* 82(1974):233–59.

Suppes, Patrick. "The Uses of Computers in Education." *Scientific American*, September 1966, pp. 207–20.

Tickton, Sidney G., ed. *To Improve Learning: An Evaluation of Instructional Technology.* Vol. 1. New York: Bowker, 1970.

Tobias, Sigmund. "Dimensions of Teachers' Attitudes toward Instructional Media." *American Educational Research Journal* 5(1968):91–98.

_____. "Lack of Knowledge and Fear of Automation as Factors in Teachers' Attitudes toward Programed Instruction and Other Media." *AV Communications Review* 14(1966):99-109.

_____. "Teachers' Attitudes toward Programed Instructional Terms." *Journal of Programed Instruction*, Fall 1963, pp. 25-29.

Trillin, Calvin. "A Public Hearing on the Origin of Species." *New Yorker*, 6 January 1973, pp. 55-58.

Turner, Donald F. "The Patent System and Competitive Policy." *New York University Law Review* 44(1969):450-76.

United States Office of Education. *Focus on Innovation: a Report on the Status and Operation of ESEA Title III, Fiscal Year 1969*. Washington, D.C.: Government Printing Office, 1971.

Vanier, Dinoo J. *Market Structure and the Business of Book Publishing*. New York: Pitman, 1973.

Wade, Nicholas. "Creationists and Evolutionists: Confrontation in California." *Science*, 17 November 1972, pp. 724–29.

Weiler, Daniel. *A Public School Voucher Demonstration: The First Year at Alum Rock*. Vol. 4. Santa Monica, Calif.: Rand Corporation, 1974.

Winn, Ira J. "Change and Resistance to the New Social Studies." *School and Society* 99(1971):182–90.

Zinn, Karl L. "Computer Technology for Teaching and Research on Instruction." *Review of Educational Research* 37(1967):618–34.

Unpublished Materials

Baldridge, J. Victor. "The Impact of Individuals, Organizational Structure, and Environment on Organizational Innovation." Research and Development Memo Number 124. (ED 091 856) 1974.

_____, and Johnson, Rudolph. "The Impact of Educational R&D Centers and Laboratories: An Analysis of Effective Organizational Strategies." (ED 079 860) 1973.

California Department of Education. "Draft Preliminary Guidelines for Learner Verification." Mimeographed. Sacramento: California Department of Education, 1974.

Cole, Henry P. "One Laboratory's Attempt at Transforming Educational Practice." (ED 051 533) 1970.

Filep, Robert T. "The Impact of Research on Utilization of Media for Educational Purposes." (ED 042 064) 1970.

_____, National Center for Educational Technology. Letter of 3 June 1973 incorporated in 21 June 1973 memorandum to NAVA Legislative Committee from Kenton Pattie, Vice President and Educational Director, National Audio-Visual Association, Inc.

Final Report of Consultants to the Director and the National Council on Educational Research. "R&D Funding Policies of the National Institute of Education: Review and Recommendations." Mimeographed. Washington, D.C.: National Institute of Education, 1975.

Hoehn, Lilburn Paul. "The Regional Educational Laboratories as Change Agents." Ph.D. dissertation, Michigan State University, 1967.

Hutchins, C.L. "Educational Development Case Study: An Elementary Science Information Unit." (ED 043 515) 1971.

Institute for Educational Development. "Research and Development in the Educational Materials Industries." (ED 043 232) 1971.

Klein, Susan. "Toward a Consensus on Minimum Criteria for Educational Products." Paper read at Annual Meeting of the American Educational Research Association, 21 April 1976, at San Francisco. Mimeographed.

Komoski, P. Kenneth. "Statement Before Curriculum Development and Supplemental Materials Committee of State of California, Sacramento, California, 11 July 1973." Mimeographed.

McClure, Robert. "A Pilot Project on User's Needs and Teacher Inservice Education Products." (ED 143 647) 1976.

National Institute of Education. "ERIC Fact Sheet." Mimeographed. Washington, D.C.: National Institute of Education, 1976.

_____. "Fiscal Year 1974 Supplemental Budget Justification." Mimeographed. Washington, D.C.: National Institute of Education, 1974.

_____, Curriculum Development Task Force. "Current Issues, Problems, and Concerns in Curriculum Development." Mimeographed. Washington, D.C.: National Institute of Education, 1976.

National Science Foundation. "Policies for the Distribution of Publications and Other Materials Developed Under the Science Education Programs of the National Science Foundation." Mimeographed. Washington, D.C.: National Science Foundation, 1975.

Naylor, David T. "Can 'The New Social Studies' Survive in the Public Schools?: A Case Study of the Perceptions of Significant School-Related Groups Regarding Nationalistic Instruction." Paper read at the National Council for the Social Studies College and University Session, November 1973. (ED 087 681) 1974.

1973 10 K Report of Harcourt Brace Jovanovich, Inc.

Papert, Seymour. "Teaching Children Thinking." Artificial Intelligence Memo Number 247. (ED 077 241) 1973.

_____. "Teaching Children to be Mathematicians vs. Teaching About Mathematics." Artificial Intelligence Memo Number 249. (ED 077 243) 1973.

_____. "Uses of Technology to Enhance Education." Artificial Intelligence Laboratory, LOGO Memo Number 8. Mimeographed. Cambridge, Mass.: Massachusetts Institute of Technology, 1973.

Rafky, David M., and Beckerman, Marvin. "Teachers' Acceptance of Innovations: Self-Interest, Altruism, and Professionalization." (ED 079 267) 1971.

"Report of Actions Taken by the State Board of Education, September 1972." Mimeographed. Sacramento: California State Board of Education, 1972.

Sanderson, Barbara A., and Kratochvil, Daniel W. "Science—A Process Approach, Product Development Report Number 8." (ED 064 066) 1971.

"Science Framework for California Schools." Sacramento: State Board of Education, 1970.

Sikorski, Linda. "A Study of the Current Status of the Implementation of Science and Mathematics Materials at the Pre-College Level in the Natural Sciences, Social Sciences, and Mathematics." (ED 129 622) 1976.

Stern, Carolyn, and Keislar, Evan R. "Teacher Attitudes and Attitude Change." (ED 109 072) 1975.

"Strengthening Instruction in Academic Subjects, Title III, Part A National Defense Education Act as Amended, Annual Report: Fiscal Year 1972." (ED 082 382) 1973.

Tucker, Marc; Harahan, Mary; Kelly, Berlin; Mason, Ward; and Yanofsky, Saul. "Building Capacity for Renewal and Reform: An Initial Report on Knowledge Production and Utilization in Education." (ED 087 095) 1973.

Turnbull, Brenda; Thorn, Lorraine; and Hutchins, C.L. "Promoting Change in Schools." (ED 090 679) 1974.

United States Office of Education, Division of Education Laboratories, Bureau of Research. "A Progress Report on the Twenty Education Laboratories." Mimeographed. Washington, D.C.: United States Office of Education, 1967.

Legal Materials

Gottschalk v. Benson, 409 U.S. 63 (1972).

Brown v. Board of Education, 347 U.S. 483 (1954).

The Telephone Cases, 126 U.S. 1 (1888).

Baker v. Selden, 101 U.S. 99 (1879).

O'Reilly v. Morse, 15 U.S. (How.) 62 (1853).

Morrissey v. Procter & Gamble Co., 379 F.2d 675 (1st Cir. 1967).

Continental Cas. Co. v. Beardsley, 253 F.2d 702 (2d Cir. 1958).

Brown Instrument Co. v. Warner, 161 F.2d 910 (D.C. Cir. 1947).

Cincinnati Traction Co. v. Pope, 210 F. 443 (6th Cir. 1913).

SmokEnders, Inc. v. Smoke No More, Inc., 184 U.S.P.Q. 309 (S.D. Fla. 1974).

Harcourt, Brace & World, Inc. v. Graphic Controls Corp., 329 F. Supp. 517 (S.D.N.Y. 1971).

Norton Printing Co. v. Augustana Hospital, 155 U.S.P.Q. 133 (N.D. Ill. 1967).

Johnson v. Duquesne Light Co., 29 F.2d 784 (W.D. Pa. 1928).

Williams & Wilkins Co. v. United States, 487 F.2d 1345 (Ct. Claims 1973), *aff'd by an equally divided court*, 420 U.S. 376 (1975).

Application of Johnston, 502 F.2d 765 (C.C.P.A. 1974), *rev'd sub. nom.* Dann v. Johnston, 425 U.S. 219 (1976).

In re Royka & Martin, 180 U.S.P.Q. 580 (C.C.P.A. 1974).

In re Miller, 164 U.S.P.Q. 46 (C.C.P.A. 1969).

Ex parte Gwin, 112 U.S.P.Q. 439 (P.O. Bd. Apps. 1955).

Ex parte Mayne, 59 U.S.P.Q. 342 (P.O. Bd. Apps. 1943).

Peter W. v. San Francisco Unified School District, 60 Cal. App. 3d 814, 131 Cal. Rptr. 854 (1st Dist. 1976) *hearing denied*, 29 September 1976.

Leeper v. State, 103 Tenn. 500, 53 S.W. 962 (1899).

Northshore School District No. 417 v. Kinnear, 84 Wash. 2d 685, 530 P. 2d 178 (1974).

Copyright Revision Act of 1976, Public Law Number 94-553, §§ 102, 107, 90 Statutes at Large 2541 (to be codified as 17 U.S.C. §§ 102(a), 102(b), 107 [Supp. 1978]).

Elementary and Secondary Education Act of 1965, Public Law Number 89-10, 79 Statutes at Large 27 *et seq.* (current version at 20 U.S.C. § 236 *et seq.* [1970 & Supp. 1977]).

National Defense Education Act of 1958, Public Law Number 85-864, Title III, § 313, as added Public Law Number 90-575, § 304(b), 82 Statutes at Large 1054 (current version at 20 U.S.C. § 453(a)(1) [1970]).

National Defense Education Act of 1958, Public Law Number 85-864, §§ 701, 731, 72 Statutes at Large 1595 (current version at 20 U.S.C. §§ 541, 551 [1970]).

National Defense Education Act of 1958, Public Law Number 83-864, Title XI, § 1101, as added Public Law Number 88-665, Title IX, § 901(a), 78 Statutes at Large 1107 (current version at 20 U.S.C. § 591 [1970]).

Education Amendments of 1972, Public Law Number 92-318, Title III, § 301(a)(2), 86 Statutes at Large 326 (current version at 20 U.S.C. §§ 1221a, 1221e [1970 & Supp. 1977]).

National Science Foundation Act of 1950, Public Law Number 507, § 3(a)(1), 64 Statutes at Large 149 (current version at 42 U.S.C. § 1862(d) [1970]).

Internal Revenue Code § 174.

Cooperative Research Act, Public Law Number 531, 68 Statutes at Large 533 (1954) (repealed 1975).

H.R. 4916, 92d Congress, 1st Session, 117 Congressional Record 3871 (1971).

H.R. 16572, 92d Congress, 2d Session, 118 Congressional Record 29970 (1972).

S. 1480, 94th Congress, 1st Session, 120 Congressional Record 6226 (1975).

Hearings Before Subcommittee on Education of the Senate Committee on Labor and Public Welfare, 88th Congress, 1st Session (1963) (statement of Maurice B. Mitchell).

Educational Technology: Hearings on H.R. 4916 Before the Select Subcommittee on Education of the House Committee on Education and Labor, 92d Congress, 2d Session 15(1972) (statement by Representative John Brademas).

Copyright Law Revision: Hearings on S. Res. 56 on S. 1361 Before the Subcommittee on Patents, Trademarks and Copyrights of the Senate Committee on the Judiciary, 93rd Congress, 1st Session 184(1973) (statement by Harold E. Wigren).

National Science Foundation Curriculum Development and Implementation for Pre-College Science Education, Report Prepared for the House Committee on Science and Technology, 94th Congress, 1st Session (1975).

California Education Code
§ 7504 (West Supp. 1977)
§ 8505 (West 1975)
§ 9202 (West 1975)
§ 9234 (West 1975)
§ 9263 (West Supp. 1977)
§ 9402 (West Supp. 1977)
§ 9426 (West 1975)
§ 9462 (West 1975)
§ 9600 (West 1975)
§ 10938 (West Supp. 1977)
§ 13487 (West Supp. 1977)

Florida Statutes Annotated
§ 233.25 (West 1977)
§ 229.57 (2)(b) (West 1977)

Indiana Constitution, Article 8, Section 1.

Michigan Statutes Annotated § 15.2085(11)(1)(a) (1975).

Hearings Before the California Senate Education Committee, 8 October 1974 (statement by Armin Rosencranz).

Treasury Regulations § 1.174–2(a) (1974).

Revenue Rulings 395, 1973–2 C.B. 87.

"Material Not Subject to Copyright." 37 Code of Federal Regulations § 202.1 (c) (1977).

"Institutional Patent Agreements." 45 Code of Federal Regulations § 650.8(c) (1976).

"Greater Rights Determination After Disclosure." 45 Code of Federal Regulations § 650.9(c)(1) (1976).

"Availability of Inventions to the Public," 45 Code of Federal Regulations § 650.11 (1976).

"Notice of Education Statement of Policy," 30 Federal Register 9408 (1965).

"Copyright Guidelines: Notice of Issuance of Guidelines on Authorizing Copyright Protection for Materials Developed Under Project Grants and Contracts," 35 Federal Register 7317 (1970).

5 California Administrative Code §§ 435–36 (1976).

President's Message to Congress on Education Reform, 6 *Weekly Compilation of Presidential Documents* 304 (3 March 1970).

Answer of defendant, Xerox Corp. and American Association for the Advancement of Science v. Sigma Scientific, Inc., Index No. 72 Civ. 954 R.O. (S.D.N.Y.).

American Law Institute. *Restatement of the Law of Torts*. 1st ed. St. Paul, Minn.: American Law Institute, 1938.

Loewen v. Turnipseed, Index No. GC 75–147–S (N.D. Miss.).

Index

About the Author

Paul Goldstein is professor of law at Stanford University. He received the B.A. from Brandeis University in 1964, and the LL.B. from Columbia University, School of Law, in 1967. From 1967 to 1975, Professor Goldstein was on the faculty of the School of Law, State University of New York at Buffalo. He joined the Stanford Law School faculty in 1975. Professor Goldstein is the author of a textbook, *Copyright, Patent, Trademark and Related State Doctrines* and of several articles on topics in intellectual property law and on the role of law in scientific and technological advance.